The Maides Revenge. A tragedy. As it hath been acted with good applause at the private house in Drury Lane, by her Majesties Servants.

James Shirley

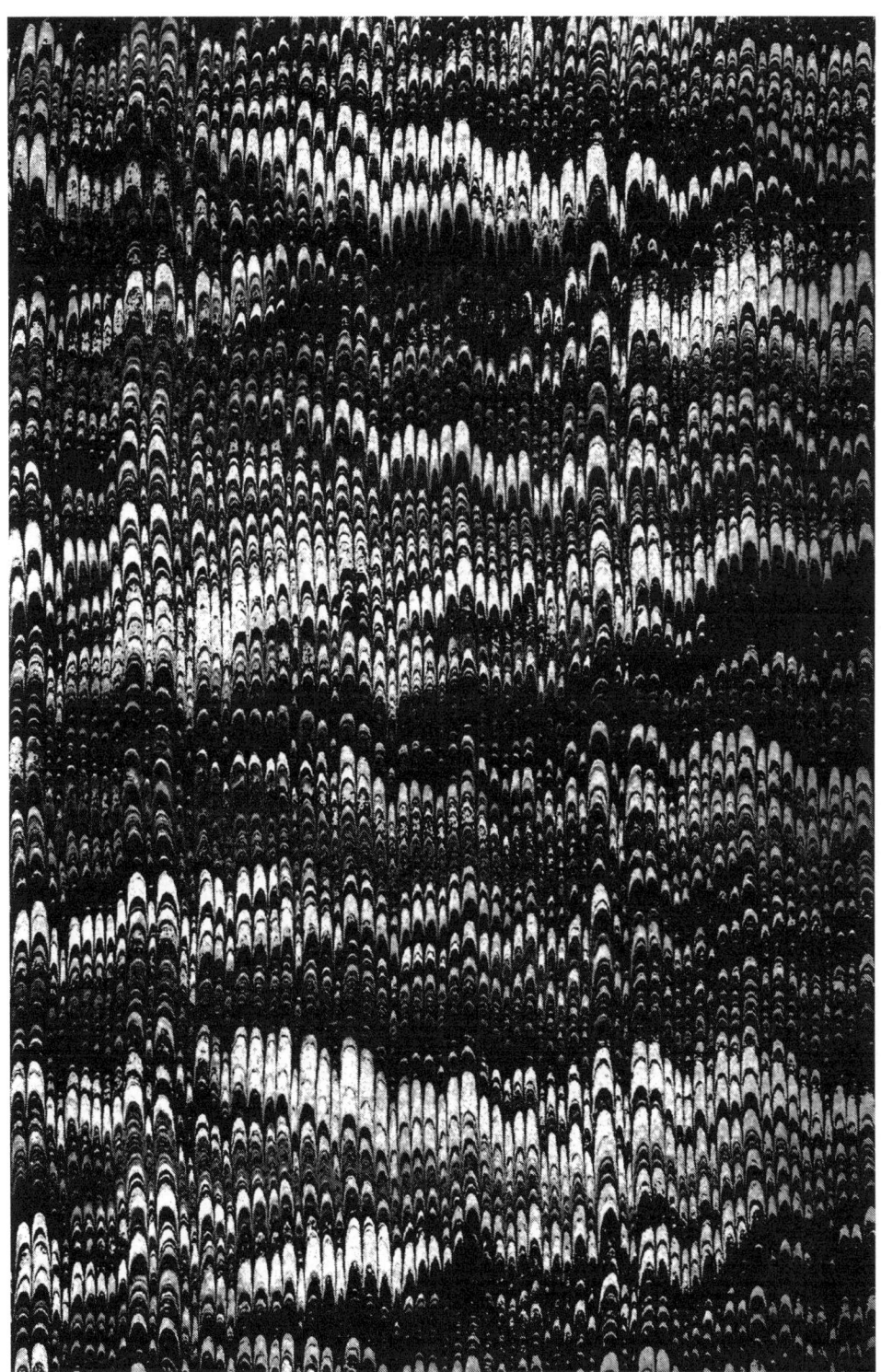

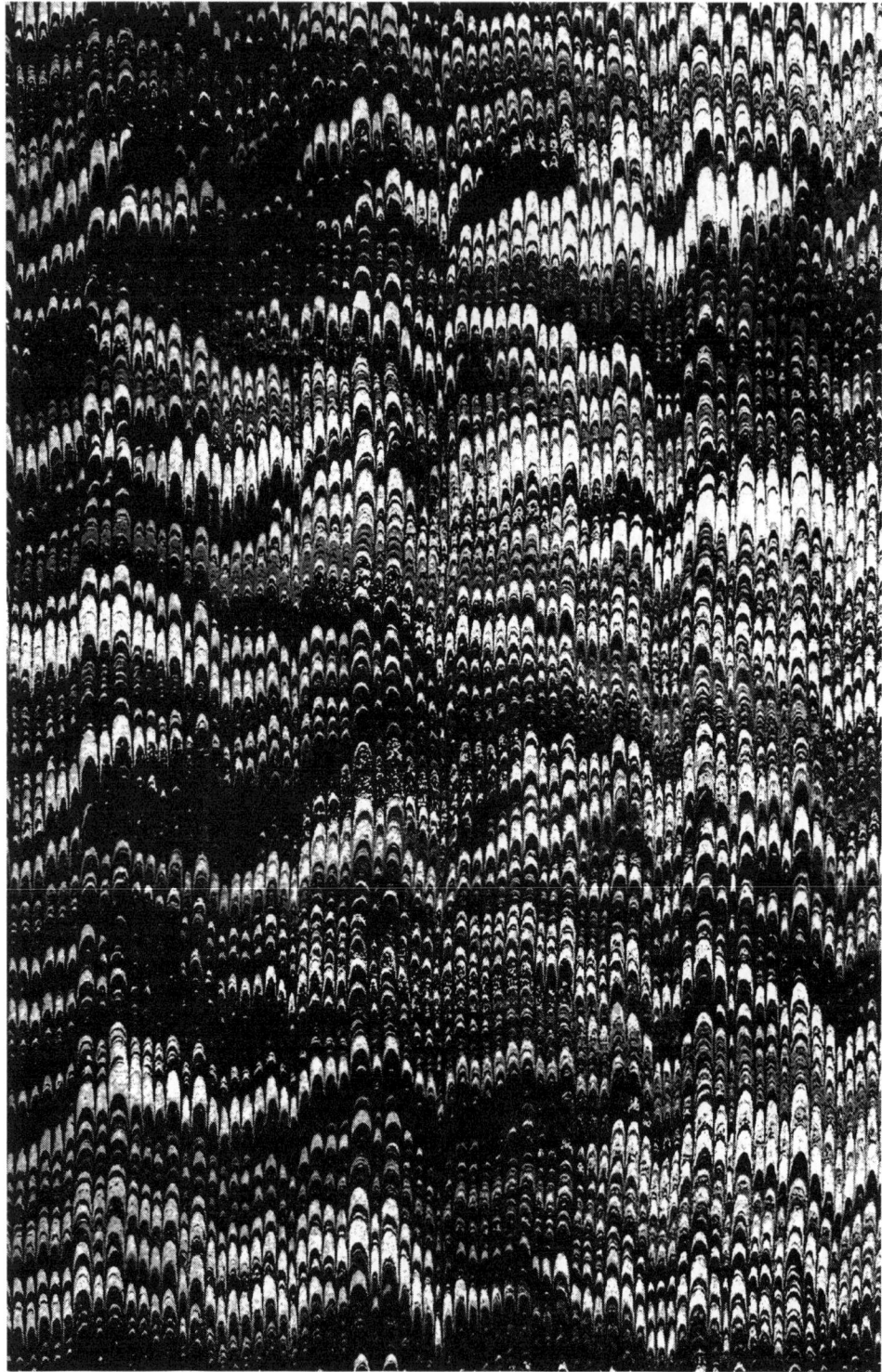

644. C. 57

THE
MAIDES
REVENGE.

A TRAGEDY.

As it hath beene Acted with good
Applaufe at the private houfe in *Drury
Lane*, by her Majefties Servants.

Written by IAMES SHIRLEY Gent.

LONDON.

Printed by *T.C.* for *William Cooke*, and are to be
fold at his fhop at *Furnivalls Inne* Gate in
Holbourne. 1639.

The Actors names.

GAsper De Vilarezo, *an old Count, Father to* Sebastiano, Catalina *and* Berinthia.

Sebastiano, *sonne to* Vilarezo.

Antonio *a lover of* Berinthia, *and friend to* Sebastiano.

Valindras *a kinsman of* Antonio.

Sforza, *a blunt Souldier.*

Valasco, *a lover of* Berinthia.

Count de monte nigro, *a braggard.*

Diego, *Servant to* Antonio.

Signior Sharkino, *a shirking Doctor.*

Scarabeo, *a Servant to* Sharkino.

Catalina ⎱
Berinthia ⎰ *Daughters to* Vilarezo.

Castabella, *Sister to* Antonio.

Ansilva, *a waiting gentlewoman to the two Sister.*

Nurse.

Servants.

TO THE WORTHILY

Honoured, *Henry Osborne* Esquire.

SIR,

TILL I be able to give you a better proofe of my
service, let not this oblation be despised. It is a
Tragedy which received encouragement and
grace on the *English* Stage; and though it
come late to the Impression, it was the second birth in this kinde, which I dedicated
to the Scene, as you have Art to distinguish; you have mercy
and a smile, if you finde a Poem infirme through want of
age, and experience the mother of strength. It is many yeares
since I see these papers, which make haste to kisse your hand;
if you doe not accuse the boldnesse and pride of them; I will
owne the child, and beleeve Tradition so farre, that you will
receive no dishonour by the acceptance; I never affected the
wayes of flattery: some say I have lost my preferment, by
not practising that Court sinne; but if you dare beleeve, I
much honour you, nor is it upon guesse, but the taste and
knowledge of your abilitie and merit; and while the Court
wherein you live, is fruitfull with Testimonies of your mind,
my Character is seal'd up, when I have said that your vertue
hath taken up a faire lodging. Read when you have leasure,
and let the Author be fortunate to be knowne.

Your Servant,

IAMES SHIRLEY.

A 2

A Catalogue of such things as hath beene Published by *James Shirley* Gent.

Traytor.
Witty Faire one.
Bird in a Cage.
Changes, or Love in a Maze.
Gratefull Servant.
Wedding.
Hide Parke.
Young Admirall.
Lady of Pleasure.
Gamster.
Example.
Dukes Mistresse.
Ball.
Chabot Admirall of France.
Royall Master.
Schoole of Complements.
Contention for Honour and Riches.
Triumph of peace, a Masque.
Maides Revenge.

Sufficient preparation. *Ant.* Had

I have not so much choise *Sebastiano*,

But if one Sister of *Antonios*,

May have a commendation to your thoughts,

I will not spend much Art in praysing her,

Her vertue speake it selfe, I shall be happy,

And be confirmd your brother, though I misse

Acceptance at *Avero*.

  Seb. Still you out doe me, I could never wish

My service better plac'd at opertunity.

Ile visit you at *Elvas*, i'th meane time

Lets hast to *Avero*, where with you Ile bring

My double welcome, and not faile to second

Any designe.

  Ant. You shall teach me a lesson

Against we meete at *Elvas* Castle sir. *Exeunt.*

    Enter Gaspar de Vilarezo, and a Servant.

  Vil. What gallants sirs are they newly entred?

  Ser. Count *de Monte Nigro* my Lord, and *Don Valasco*,

  Vil. Give your observance then, I know their busineffe,

Catalina and *Berinthia* are the starrs

Direct them hither, *Gaspars* house shall give

Respect to all, but they are two such Iewels,

I must dispose maturely, I should else

Returne ingratitude upon the heavens

For leaving me such pledges, nor am I,

Like other fathers carried with the streame

Of love toth youngest, as they were in birth,

They had my tendernesse, *Catalina* then

Is eldest in my care, *Berinthia*

Her childs part too, both faire and vertuous,

But daughters are held losses to a family,

Sonnes onely to maintaine honour and stemme

Alive in their posterity, and I now thinke on't,

My sonne *Sebastiano* hath beene slow

In his returne from *Lisbone*, oh that boy

Renewes my age with hope, and hath returnd

My.

My care in education, weight for weight
With noble quality, well belov'd byth best
Oth Dons in *Spaine* and *Portugall*, whose loves
Do often stretch his absence to such length
As this hath beene.

Enter Count de monte Nigro, and Catalina.

But heres my eldest daughter
With her amorous Count, Ile not be seene, *Exit.*

Cata. You have beene absent long my noble Count,
Beshrew me but I dreamt on you last night.

Count. Ha ha, did you so, Tickle her in her sleep I perceive,
Sweete Lady I did but like the valiant beast,
Give a little ground, to returne with a greater
Force of love, now by my fathers sword
And gauntlet thart a pretious peece of vertue,
But prethee what didst dreame of me last night?

Cata. Nay twas an idle dreame, not worth the repitition.

Count. Thou dreamst I warrant thee, that I was fighting
For thee up to the knees in blood, why I dare doo't,
Such dreames are common with Count *de monte*
Nigro, my sleepes are nothing else but rehearsals of
Battels, and wounds, and ambuscadoes, *Donzell Delphebe*
Was a Mountebanke of vallour, *Rosicheere* a puffe,
My dreames deserve to be ith Chronicles.

Cata. Why, now my dreame is out. *Count.* What?

Cata. I dreamt that you were fighting. *Count.* So,

Cata. And that in single combate, for my sake
You slew a giant, and you no sooner had
Rescued my honour, but there crept a pigmee
Out of the earth, and kild you.

Count. Very likely, the valliantst man must dye.

Cata. What by a pigmee?

Count. I, thats another giant, I remember *Hercules*
Had a conflict with'em, oh my *Dona*
Catalina I well would I were so happy once to
Maintaine some honourable duell for thy sake, I shall
Nere be well, till I have kild some body, fight, tis true

I

I have never yet fleſht my ſelfe in blood, no body
Would quarell with me, but I finde my ſpirit prompt
If occaſion would but winke at me, why not? wherefore has
Nature given me theſe brawny armes, this manly bulke,
And theſe Colloſſian ſupporters, nothing but to ſling
The ſledge, or pitch the bare, and play with
Axletrees ; if thou loveſt me, do but command me
Some worthy ſervice; pox a dangers, I weigh 'em no
More than fleabitings, would ſome body did hate that
Face, now I wiſh it with all my heart.

  Cata. Would you have any body hate me?

  Conn. Yes, Ide hate 'em, Ide but thruſt my hand into their
Mouth downe to the bottome of their bellies, plucke
Out their lungs and ſhake their inſides outward.

        Enter Berinthia and Valaſco.

  Ber. Noble Sir, you neede not heapē more proteſtations,
I do beleeve you love me.

  Val. Doe you beleeve I love, and not accept it?

  Ber. Yes I accept it too, but apprehend me
As men doe guifts, whoſe acceptation does not
Binde to performe what every giver craves ;
Without a ſtaine to virgin modeſty
I can accept your love, but pardon mē,
It is beyond my power to grant your ſuitē.

  Val. Oh you too much ſubject a naturall guift,
And make your ſelfe beholding for your owne :
The Sunne hath not more right to his owne beames,
With which he gildes the day, nor the Sea lord
Of his owne waves.

  Ber. Alaſſe, what iſt to ownē a paſſion
Without power to direct it, for I move,
Not by a motion I can call my owne,
But by a higher rapture, in obedience
To a father, and I havē yet no freedome
To place affection, ſo you but endeere me
Without a merit.

  Cata. Heres my ſiſter.

Cou. And *Don Valasco*, how now, are thy arrowes feathred?

Val. Well enough for roving.

Count. Roving, I thought so.

Val. But I hope faire.

Count. Shoote home then ; *Valasco* I have
Presented my mistris with a paper of verses, see she
Is reading of 'em.

Val. Didst make 'em thy selfe.

Cou. My money did, what an idle question is that? as tho wē
That are great men, are not furnished with stipendary
Muses, I am sure for my owne part I can buy 'em
Cheaper than I can make 'em a great deale, would
You have learning have no reward, she laughs
At 'em, I am glad of that.

Ber. They savour of a true Poeticke fury.

Count. Do you smell nothing, something hath some savour.

Cata. But this line my thinks hath more feete than the rest.

Cou. It sho'd run the better for that Lady, I did it a purpose.

Cata. But heres another lame.

Count. That was my conceit, my owne invention, lame
Halting verses, theres the greatest Art, besides I
Thereby give you to understand, that I am valiant,
Dare cut of legs and armes at all times, and make 'em
Goe halting home that are my enemies, I am
An Iambographier, now it is out.

Cata. For honours sake what's that?

Count. One of the sourest versifiers that ever crept out of
Pernassus when I set on't, I can make any body hang himselfe
With pure Iambicks, I can fetch blood with *Ascelpiads*
Sting, with *Phalenciums* whip, with *Saphicks*
Bastinado, with hexameter and pentameter, and
Yet I have a trimeter left for thee my *Dona Catalina.*

Ber. Conclude a peace sir with your passion,
I am sory love hath beene unkind to you,
To point at me, who, till she first have knit
The sacred knot of marriage, am forbid
To thinke of love.

Val.

Vila. Come let us in, my house spreads to receive you,
Which you may call your owne, Ile leade the way.

Cata. Please you walke Sir.

Ant. It will become me thus to waite on you.　　*Exeunt,*
　　　　　　　　　　　　manet Count, and Valasco.

Count. Does not the foole ride us both?

Val. What foole? both, whom?

Count. That foole, both us, we are but horses and may
Walke one another for ought I see before the doore, when he
Is alight and entred. I do not relish that same
Novice, he were not best gull me; harke you Don
Valasco, what shals doe?

Val. Doe, why?

Count. This *Antonio* is a sutor to one of 'em.

Val. I feare him not.

Coun. I do not feare him neither, I dare fight with him, and
He were ten *Antonios,* but the Ladies *Don,* the Ladies,

Val. Berinthia, to whom
I pay my love devotions, in my eare
Seemd not to welcome him, your Lady did.

Count. I but for all that he had most mind to your mistris,
And I do not see but if he pursue it,
There is a possibility to scale the fort, Ladies
Mindes may alter, by your favour, I have lesse
Cause to feare o'th two; if he love not *Catalina*
My game is free, and I may have a course in
Her Parke the more easily.

Val. Tis true, he preferred service to *Berinthia,*
And what is she then to resist the vowes
Antonio if he love, dare heape upon her?
He's gracious with her father, and a friend
Deere as his bosome to *Sebastiano,*
And may be is directed by that brother
To aime at her, or if he make free choyce,
Berinthias beauty will draw up his soule.

Count. And yet now I thinke on't, he was very sawcy
With my love to support her arme, which she

Accepted too familiarly, and she should
But love him, it were as bad for me, for tho he care
Not for her, I am sure she will never abide me after it,
By this hilts I must kill him, theres no remedy,
I cannot helpe it.

   Val. Ile know my destiny.
   Count. And I my fate, but here he comes.   *Enter Antonio.*
   Ant. The strangest resolution of a father
I ever heard, I was covetous
To acquaint him with my wishes, praid his leave
I might be servant to *Berinthia*,
But thus he briefly answered, untill
His eldest daughter were dispos'd in marriage
His youngest must not love, and therefore wisht me,
Vnlesse I could place *Catalina* here,
Leave off soliciting, yet I was welcome,
But fed on nothing but *Berinthia*,
From whose faire eyes love threw a thousand flames
Into *Antonios* heart, her cheeks bewraying
As many amorous blushings, which brake out
Like a forc'd lightning from a troubled cloud,
Discovering a restraint, as if within
She were at conflict, which her colour onely
Tooke liberty to speake, but soone fell backe,
And as it were checkt by silence.
   Con. Ile stay no longer, sir a word with you, are you desperat?
   Ant. Desperate, why sir?
   Connt. I aske and you be desperate, are you weary of your
Life, and you be, say but the word; some body can tell
How to dispatch you without a physitian, at a minuits
   warning.
   Anto. You are the noble Count *de monte Nigro.*
   Connt. I care not a Spanish fig what you count me, I must
Call you to account sir; in briefe the Lady
Dona Catalina is my mistris, I do not meane to be baffled
While this toole has any steele in't, and I have some
Mettall in my selfe too.

                                  Ant.

Ant. The *Dona Catalina* ? do you love her ?   *Enter Vila,*
She is a Lady in whom onely lives   *Sebaſt. Cata, Ber.*
Natures and Arts perfection, borne to ſhame
All former beauties, and to be the wonder
Of all ſucceeding, which ſhall fade and wither
When ſhe is but remembred.

  Count. I can endure no more, Diablo, he is mortally in love
With *Catalina.*

  Vala. Tis ſo, he's tane with *Catalinaes* beautie.

  Count. Sir I am a ſervant of that Lady, therefore eate up
Your words, or you ſhall be ſenſible that I am Count
De monte Nigro, and ſhe's no diſh for *Don Antonio.*

  Ant. Sir I will do you right.

  Count. Or I will right my ſelfe.

  Cata. He did direct thoſe prayſes unto me
This doth confirme it.

  Ber. He cannot ſo ſoone alter,
I ſhall diſcover a paſſion through my eye

  Count. Thou ſheweſt thy ſelfe a noble Gentleman, the
Count is now thy friend.

  Ant. Does it become me ſir, to proſecute
Where ſuch a noble Count is intereſſed,
Vpon my ſoule I wiſh the Lady yours,
Here my ſuite fals, with tender of my ſervice;
Would you were married, nay in bed together,
My honourable Count.

  Cata. Your face is cloudy ſir, as you ſuſpected
Your preſence were not welcome; had you naught
But title of a brothers friendſhip, it were
Enough to oblige us to you, but your worth
In *Catalinaes* eies, bids me proclaime you
A double acceptation.

  Ant. Oh you are bounteous Ladie.

  Count. Sir —

  Ant. Doe not feare me,
I am not worthie your opinion,
It ſhall be happineſſe for me to kiſſe

This Ivory hand.

Count. The whilst I kisse her lip and be immotall.

Seb. Antonio my father is a rocke,
In that he first resolved, and I account it part of my
Owne unhappinesse, I hope you hold me not suspected.

Ant. I were unworthy such a friend, his care
Becomes him nobly ; has not younder Count
Some hope of *Catalina.*

Seb. My father thinkes that sister worthy of
More than a bare Nobility.

Ant. Ile backe to *Eluas* noble sir,
This entertainement is so much above
Antonios merit, if I leave you not
I shall be out of hope to——

Vila. Nay then you mocke me sir, you must not leave me
Without discourtesie so soone, we trifle time,
This night you are my guest, my honored Count,
My Don *Valasco.*

Count. Yes my Lord, wee'le follow.

Ant. Ha I am resolv'd, like Barge-men when they row,
Ile looke auother way then that I goe.   *Exeunt.*

Actus 2. Scæna I.

Enter *Catalina* and *Ansilva.*

Cata. ANd you observe with curious eye
All Gentlemen that come hither, whats your
Of *Don Antonio?*   (opinion.

Ans. My opinion Madam, I want Art.
To judge of him.

Cata. Then without Art your judgement.

Ans. He is one of the most accomplisht Gentlemen
Ansilva ere beheld, pardon Madam.

Cata. Nay, it doth not displease, yare not alone,
He hath friends to second you, and who dost thinke
Is cause he tarrries here.

Ans. Your noble father will not let him goe.

Cata. And canſt thou ſee no higher? then thou art dull.

Anſ. Madam, I gueſſe at ſomething more.

Cata. What?

Anſ. Love?

Cata. Of whom?

Anſ. I know not that.

Cata. How not that? Thou'dſt bring thy former truth
Into ſuſpition, why tis more apparant
Then that he loves.

Anſ. If judging eyes may guide him,
I know where he ſhould'chuſe, but I have heard
That love is blind.

Cata. Ha?   (not his

Anſ. Vertue would direct him Madam unto you, I know
Obedience, I ſhall repent if I offend.

Cata. Tha'rt honeſt, be yet more free, hide not a thought
that may concerne it.

Anſ. Then Madam I thinke he loves my Lady *Berinthia*;
I have obſerv'd his eyes rowle that way,
Even now I ſpied him
Cloſe with her in the Arbour, pardon me Madam.

Cata. Th'aſt done me faithfull ſervice, be yet more vigilant,
I know thou ſpeakſt all truth, I doe ſuſpect him,   *Exit Anſ.*
My ſiſter, ha? Dare ſhee maintaine contention?
Is this the dutie bindes her to obey
A fathers precepts, tis diſhonour to me.   *Enter Anſilva.*

Anſ. Madam, heres a pretty hanſome ſtripling new alight,
Enquires for *Don Antonio*.

Cata. Let me ſee him, 'twill give mē good occaſion to be
My owne obſerver;   *Enter Diego.*
Whom would you ſir?

Die. I am ſent in queſt of *Antonio*.

Cata. He ſpeakes like a Knight errant, he comēs in queſt.

Die. I have heard it a little vertue in ſome Spanniels, to
Queſt now and then Lady.

Cata. But you are none.

Die. My Mr. cannot beate me from him Madam, I am one of
The oldeſt appurtenances belonging to him, and yet I

Have little moſſe in my chinne.

Cata. The more to come, a wittie knave.

Die. No more wit then will keep my head warme, I beſeech you amiable Virgin help my Maſter *Antonio* to ſome intelligence that a ſervant of his waits to ſpeake with him from his ſiſter *Madona Caſtabella.*

Cata. It ſhall not neede ſir, Ile give him noticē my ſelfe, *Anſilva* Entertaine time with him. *Exit.*

Anſ. A promiſing young man.

Die. Doe you waite on this Lady ?

Anſ. Yes ſir.

Die. Wee are both of a tribe then, though wēe differ in our ſexe, I beſeech you taxe me not of immodeſty, or want of breeding, that I did not ſalute you upon the fiſt view of your perſon, this kiſſe ſhall be as good as preſſe-mony to bind me to your ſervice.

Anſ. 'Yare very welcome, by my virginity. *Exit.*

Die. Your virginitie a good word to ſave an oath, for all ſhe made me a curſie, it was not good manners to leave mee ſo ſoone 'yare very welcome by my virginity ; was ſhe afraid of breaking, it may be ſhe is crack'd already, but here ſhe is againe. *Enter Anſilva.*

Anſ. May I begge your name ſir ?

Die. No begger ſweet, would you have it at length, then My name is Signior *Baltazaro Clere Mautado,* But for brevities ſake they call me *Diego.*

Anſ, Then Signior *Diego* once more you are welcome.

Die. *Bazelez manes Signiora,* and what my tongue is not able to expreſſe, my head ſhall; it ſeemes you have liv'd long a Virgin.

Anſ. Not above ſeven or eight and thirty yēarēs.

Die. By Lady a tried Virgin, you have given the world A large teſtimony of your virginity.

Enter Ant, Berin, and Catal.

Ber. I ſhould be thus a diſobediēnt daughter A Fathers Heſts are ſacred.

Ant. But in love They have no power, it is but tyranny,

Plainē

Plaine ufurpation to command the minde
Againft its owne election ; I am yours,
Vow'd yours for ever, fend me not away
Shipwrack'd ith' habour, fay but you can love me,
And I will waite an age, not wifh to move
But by commiffion from you, to whom
I render the poffeffion of my felfe :
Ha ? we are betrai'd, I muft ufe cunning,
She lives in you, and take not in worfe fence,
You are more gracious, in that you are
So like your eldeft fifter, in whom lives
The coppy of fo much perfection,
All other feeme to imitate.

 Cata. Does he not praife me now ?

 Ant. But here fhe is,
Madam, not finding you ith' garden,
I met this Lady.

 Cata. I came to tell you
A fervant of yours attends with letters from
Your fifter *Madona Caftabella.*

 Ant. Diego what newes ?

 Die. Sir, my Lady remembers her love, thefe letters in-
forme you the ftate of all things.

 Cata. What ferious conference had you fifter with that
Gentleman.

 Ber. Would you had heard them fifter, they concern'd
your Commendations.

 Cata. Why fhould he not deliver them to my felfe.

 Ber. It may be then
You would have thought he flattered.

 Cata. I like not this rebound,
Tis faireft to catch at fall.

 Ber. Sifter, I hope
You have no fufpition, I have courted
His ftay or language on my life no accent
Fell from me, your owne eare would not have heard
With acceptation,

 Cata. It may be fo, and yet I dare acquit you,

In duty to a Father, you would wish me
All due respect, I know it.

Ant. Diego.   *Die.* Sir.

Ant. You observe the waiting creatures in the blacke,
Harke, you apprehend me.   *Whisper.*

Die. With as much tenacity as a servant.

Cat. I hope sir, now we shall enjoy you longer.

Ant. The gods would sonner be sicke with *Nectar*, than
Grow weary of such faire societie ;   *(Antonio*
But I am at home expected, a poore sister,
My fathers care alive, and dying was
His Legacy, having out-staid my time
Is tender of my absence.

    Enter Vilarezo, Sebastiano, Count, and Valasco.

Cata. My Lord *Antonio* meanes to take his leave.

Vila. Although last night you were inclin'd to goe,
Let us prevaile this morning.

Cat. A servant of his, he saies, brought letters
To hasten departure.

Vila. Why sirra, will you rob us of your master.

Die. Not guilty my Lord.

Count. Sir, if you'le needs go, we'le bring you on your way.

Ant. I humbly thank your honour, Ile not be so troublesome.

Count. Would you were gone once, I doe not meane to
trouble my selfe so much I warrant thee.

Ant. I have now a charge upon me, I hope it may
Excuse me, if I hasten my returne.

Vila. Tis faire, and reasonable, well sir, my sonne
Shall waite on you oth' way, if any occasion
Draw you to *Avero*, lets hope you'le see us,
You know your welcome.

Ant. My Lord the favours done me, would proclaime
I were too much unworthy not to visit you,
Oft as I see *Avero*; Madam I part with some unhappinesse
To lose your presence, give me leave I may
Be absent your admirer, to whose memory
I write my selfe a servant,

Count. Poxe on your complement, you were not best write

In

In her table-bookes.

Cata. You doe not know
What power you have o're me, that but to pleafe you,
Can frame my felfe to take a leave fo foone.

Vala. What thinke you of that my Lord ?

Count. Why, fhe fayes fhe has power to take her leave
So foone, no hurt ath' world in't, I hope fhe is an
Innocent Lady.   *To Berinth.*

Ant. The fhallow rivers glide away with noife,
The deepe are filent ; fare you well, Lady.

Count. I told you he is a fhallow fellow.

Vala. I know not what to thinke on't *Berinthia.*

Ant. Gentlemen happineffe and fucceffe in your defires.

Seb. Ile fee you a league or two.

Vila. By any meanes, nay fir.

Ant. Diego.

Die. My Lord I have a fuite to you before I goe.

Vila. To me *Diego*, prethee fpeake it.

Die. That while other Gentlemen are happy to devide
their affections among the Ladies, I may have your honours
leave to beare fome good-will to this Virgin : *Cupid* hath
throwne a dart at me, like a blinde buzzard as he was, and
theres no recovery without a cooler ; if I be fent into thefe
parts, I defire humbly I may be bould to rub acquaintance
with Miftreffe *Anfilva.*

Vila. With all my heart *Diego.*

Die. Madam, I hope you will not be an enemy to a poore
Flye that is taken in the flame of the blind god.

Cata. You fhall have my confent fir.

Vila. But what fayes *Anfilva*, haft thou a mind to a husband?

Anf. I feare I am too young feven yeares hence were time
enough for me.

Seb. Shees not full fortie yet fir.

Die. I honour the Antiquitie of her maidenhead, thou
Miftreffe of my heart.

Ant. Come lets away *Diego* our horfes------

Vila. We'le bring you to the gate.

Count. Yes, wee'le bring him out of doores, would wee

D   were

Were shut of him.   *Exeunt.*   *manet Ansilva.*

Ans. Hay ho, who would have thought I should have
benne in love with a stripling, have I seene so many maiden-
heades suffer before me, and must mine come to the blocke at
fortie yeares old, if this *Diego* have the grace to come on, I
shall have no power to keepe my selfe chast any longer; how
many maides have beene overrunne with this love ? but
heres my Lady.   *Exit.*

Enter Catalina and Valasco.

Cat. Sir, you love my sister.

Val. With an obedient heart.

Cat. Where do you think *Don Antonio* hath made choice
To place his love ?

Val. There where I wish it may grow older in desire,
And be crown'd with fruitfull happinesse.

Cat. Hath your affection had no deeper roote,
That tis rent up already, I had thought
It would have stood a Winter, but I see
A Summer storme hath kil'd it, fare you well sir.

Val. How's this, a Summers storme !
Lady by the honour of your birth,
Put off these cloudes, you maze me, take off
The wonder you have put upon *Valasco,*
And solve these riddles.

Cat. You love *Berinthia.*

Val. With a devoted heart, else may I die
Contempt of all mankinde, not my owne soule
Is deerer to me.

Cat. And yet you wish *Antonio* may be crown'd
With happinesse in his love, he loves *Birinthia.*

Val. How ?

Cat. Beyond expression, to see how a good nature
Free from dishonour in it selfe, is backward
To thinke another guilty, suffers it selfe
Be poisoned with opinion, did your eyes
Emptie their beames so much in admiration
Of your *Berinthias* beauty, you left none
To observe your owne abuses.

Val.

Vala. Doth not *Antonio* dedicate his thoughts
To your acceptance, 'tis impoffible,
I heard him praife you to the heavens, above 'em ;
Made himfelfe hoarfe but to repeate your vertues
As he had beene in extafie ; love *Birinthia?*
Hell is not blacker than his foule, if he
Love any goodneffe but your felfe.

  Cat. That leffon he with impudencē hath reade
To my owne eares, but fhall I tell you fir ?
We are both made but properties to raife
Him to his partiall ends, flattery is
The ftalkeing horfe of pollicy, faw you not,
How many flames he fhot into her eyes
When they were parting, for which fhe pay'd backē
Her fubtill teares, he wrung her by the hand,
Seem'd with the greatneffe of his paffion
To have beene o're borne, Oh cunning treachēry ļ
Worthy our juftice, true he commended me ;
But could you fee the Fountaine that fent forth
So many cozening ftreames, you would fay *Styx*
Were Chriftall to it, and waft not to the Count,
Whom he fuppos'd was in purfuite of mē;
Nay, whom he knew did love me, that he might
Fire him the more to confummate my marriage
That I difpofed he might have of acceffe
To his belov'd *Berinthia*, the end
Of his defires I can confirme it, he praid
To be fo happy with my fathers leave
To be her amorous fervant, which he nobly
Denied, partly expreffing your engagements ;
If you have leaft fufpition of this truth:
But dee' thinke fhe love you?

  Val. I cannot challenge her, but fhe has lēt fall
Something to make me hope, how thinke you fheé's
Affected to *Antonio* ?

  Cat. May be
Luke warme as yet, but foone as as fhees caught,
Inevitably his, without prevention.

For

For my owne part I hate him in whom lives
A will to wrong a Gentleman, for hee was
Acquainted with your love, 'twas my respect
To tender so your injury, I could not
Be silent in it, what you meane to doe
I leave to your owne thoughts.

   Val. Oh stay sweete Lady, leave me not to struggle
Alone with this universall affliction ;
You speake even now *Berinthia* would be his
Without prevention, oh that Antidote,
That Balsome to my wound.

   Cat. Alas I pitty you, and the more, because
I see your troubles so amaze your judgement,
Il' tell you my opinion sir'oth' sudden ;
For him, he is not worth *Valasco's* anger,
Onely thus, you shall discover to my Father,
She promis'd you her love, be confident
To say you did exchange faith to her ; this alone
May chance assure her, and if not I hav't :
Steale her away, your love I see is honourable,
So much I suffer when desert is wounded,
You shall have my assistance, you apprehend me.

   Val. I am devoted yours, command me ever.

   Cat. Keepe smooth your face, and still maintaine your wor-
With *Berinthia*, things must be manag'd   (ship
And strucke in the maturity, noble sir ; I wish
You onely fortunate in *Berinthias* love.

   Val. Words are too poore to thanke you, I looke on you
As my safe guiding starre.   *Exit.*

   Cat. But I shall prove a wandering starre, I have
A course which I must finish for my selfe.
Glide on thou subtill mover, thou hast brought
This instrument already for thy aymes,
Sister, Ile breake a Serpents egge betimes,
And teare *Antonio* from thy very bosome ;
Love is above all law of nature, blood,
Not what men call, but what that bides is good.   *Exit.*
      Enter Castabella and Villandras,

Vil. Be not so carefull Cocze, your brothers well,
Be confident if he were otherwise
You should have notice, whom hath he to share
Fortunes without you ? all his ills are made
Lesse by your bearing part, his good is doubled
By your communichaing.

   Cast. By this reason
All is not well, in that my ignorance
What fate hath hapned, barres me off the portion
Belongs to me sister, but my care
Is so much greater, in that *Diego* whom
J charg'd to put on wings, if all were well,
Is dull in his returne.   *Enter Antonio and Diego.*

   Vil. His Master happily hath commanded him
To attend him homewards, this is recompenc'd
Already, looke they are come ;
Y'are welcome sir.

   Ant. Oh sister, ere you let fall words of welcome,
Let me unlade a treasure in your care
Able to weigh downe man.

   Cast. What treasure brother, you amaze me.

   Ant. Never was man so blest,
As heavens had studied to enrich me here,
So am I fortunate.

   Vil. You make me covetous.

   Ant. I have a friend.

   Vil. You have a thousand sir, is this your treasure ?

   Ant. But I have one more worth then millions,
And he doth onely keepe alive that name
Of friendship in his breast, pardon *Villandros*,
Tis not to straine your love, whom I have tried,
My worthiest cozen.

   Cast. But where is this same friend, why came he not
To *Eluas* with you, sure he cannot be
Deare to you Brother, to whom I am not indebted
At least for you.

   Die. I have many deare friends too, my Taylor is one
To whom I am indebted.

                                            Ant.

Ant. His Commiſſion
Stretch'd not ſo farre, a Fathers tie was on him,
But I have his noble promiſe,er't be long,
We ſhall enjoy him.

Caſt. Brother I hope
You know how willingly I can entertaine
Your bliſſe,and make it mine, pray ſpeake the man
To whom we owe ſo much.

Ant. Twere not charity to ſtarve you thus with ſhaddowes,
Take him,and with him in thy boſome locke
The Mirrour of fidelity,*Don Sebaſtiano.*

Caſt. I oft have heard you name him full of worth,
And upon that relation have laid up,
One deare to my remembrance.

Ant. But he muſt be dearer *Caſtabella,*harke you ſiſter,
I have beene bold upon thy vertue, to
Invite him to you, if your heart be free.
Let it be empty ever, if he doe not
Fill it with nobleſt love,to make relation,
What zeale he gave of a worthy nature,
At our laſt parting (when betwixt a ſonne,
And friend he ſo divided his affections
And out did both) you would admire him : were
I able I would build a temple where
We tooke our leave,
The ground it ſelfe was hallowed
So much with his owne piety, *Diego* ſaw it.

Die. Yes ſir,I ſaw,and heard,and wondred.

Ant. Come I will tell you all,to your chamber ſiſter,
Diego our plot muſt on,all time is loſt
Vntill we try the mooving.

Die. If the plot pleaſe you ſir,let me alone to play my part
I warrant you.

Ant. Come *Caſtabella,*and prepare to heare
A ſtory not of length but worth your care.   *Exeunt*

      Enter *Vilarezo,Valaſco,*and *Catalina.*

Vil. You have not dealt ſo honourably ſir,
As did become you,to proceede ſo farre

                   Without

Without my knowledge, give me leave to tell you
You are not welcome.

   Val. My Lord I am forry,
If I have any way trangreft, I was not
Refpectleffe of your honour, nor my fame,
Valafco fhall be unhappy, if by him
You fhall derive a ftaine, my actions faire,
I have done nothing with *Berinthia*,
To merit fuch a language, twas not ripe,
For me to interrupt the father, when I knew not
What grace I held with her.

   Vil, Hell on her grace, is this her duty? ha,
I can forget my nature if fhe dare
Make fo foone forfeit of her piety;
Oh where is that fame awfull dread of Parent,
Should live in children; tis her ambition
To out runne her fifter, but Ile curbe her impudence,

   Cata. Retire your felfe, this paffion muft have way,
This workes as I would have it, teare nothing fir,
Obfcure.   *Exit Val.*

   Vil. He cloyfter her, and ftarve this fpirit
Makes her deceive my truft; *Catalina*
Vpon thy duty I command thee, take
Her cuftody on thee, keepe her from the eye
Of all that come to *Averro*, let her difcourfe
With pictures on the wall, I feare fhe hath
Forgot to fay her prayers, is fhe growne fenfuall?

   Cata. But my Lord.

   Vil. Oh keepe thy accents for a better caufe,
She hath contemd us both, thou canft not fee
What blemifh fhe derives unto our name.
Yet thefe are fparkes, he hath a fire within,
Will turne all into flames, wheres *Valafco*?

   Cata. Good fir, a much afflicted worthy Gentleman,
At your difpleafure.

   Vil. Thou art too full of pitty, nay th'art cruell
To thy owne fame, he muft not have acceffe.
To profecute, it was my doting finne,

Of too much confidence in *Berinthia*,
Gave her such libertie, on my blessing punish it,
Twill be a vertuous act, the snow I thought
Was not more innocent, more cold, more chaste,
Why my command bound her in ribs of ice,
But shees dissolv'd, to thee Ile leave her now,   *Exit*
Be the maintainer of thy Fathers vow.

   Val. Why I am undone now.

   Cata. Nothing lesse, this conflict
Prepares your peace, I am her guardian,
Love smiles upon you, I am not inconstant,
Having more power to assist you, but away,
We must not be discri'd, expect ere long
To heere what you desire.

   Val. My blisse I remember.   *Exit*

   Cata. *Berinthia*, y'are my prisoner, at my leisure
Ile studdy on your fate, I cannot be
Friend to my selfe, when I am kind to thee.   *Exit*

Actus. 3. Scæna. 1.

Enter Sebastiano, Berinthia, Ansilva, Diego meetes them.

Seb. **V.V**Elcome honest *Diego*, your Master *Antonio* is in
          health I hope.

   Die. He commanded me, remember his service to you, I
have obtaind his leave for a small absence to perfect a suite I
lately commenc'd in this Court.

   Seb. You follow it close me thinks *Berinthia*, I see this cloud
Vanish already, be not dejected, soone
Ile know the depth ont, should the world forsake thee,
Thou shalt not want a brother deere *Berinthia*.   *Exit*
            Secretly gives her a Letter.

   Die. This is my Lady *Berinthia*, prethee let me shew
Some manners, Madam my Master *Antonio* speakes his
Service to you in this paper: alas Madam, I was but
Halfe at home, and I am returnd to see if I can recover

                    The

The tother preece of my selfe, so, was it not a reasonable
Complement.

Ber. *Antonio*, he's constant I perceive.   *Exit*

Die. So, we are alone, sweet Mistresse *Ansilva*, I am bold
To renue my suite, which least it should either
Fall or depend too long, having past my declaration,
I shall desire to come to a judgement.
My cause craves nothing but justice,
That is, that you would be mine; and now since
Your selfe is judge also, I beseech you be not partiall
In your owne cause, but give sentence for the plaintiffe, and
I will discharge the fees of the Court on this fashion.

Enter Berinthia.

Ber. Here is a haven yet to rest my soule on,
In midst of all unhappinesse, which I looke on,
With the same comfort a distressed Sea man
A farre off, viewes the coast he would enjoy,
When yet the Seas doe tosse his reeling barke,
Twixt hope and danger, thou shalt be conceald.

She mistaking as she moved, put up the Letter, it fals downe.

Ans. Heres my Lady *Berinthia.*

Die. What care I for my Lady *Berinthia*, and she thinkes
Much, would she had one to stoppe her mouth.

Ans. But I must observe her, upon her fathers displeasure,
She is committed to my Ladies custody, who hath made
Me her keeper, she must be lockt up.

Die. Ha lockt up.

Ans. Madam, it is now time you would retire to your owne
Chamber.

Ber. Yes, prethee doe *Ansilva* in this gallery,
I breathe but too much aire, oh *Diego* youle have
An answer I perceive, ere you returne.

Die. My journey were to no purpose else Madam, I apprehend her, ile waite an opportunity, alas poore Lady, is my
sweete heart become a jaylor, there's hope of an office without money.   *Enter Ansilva hastily.*

Ans. *Diego* I spy my Lady *Catalina* comming this way, pray
shrowd your selfe behinde this cloth, I would be loath shee

E   should

should see us here together, quickely, I heare her treading.

Enter Catalina.

Cata. Ansilva.   *Ans.* Madam.

Cata. Who's with you?   *Ans.* No body Madam.

Cata. Was not *Diego* with you, *Antonioes* man?

Ans. He went from me Madam halfe an houre agoe,
To visit friends ith' City.

Cat. He hath not seene *Berinthia* I hope.

Ans. Vnlesse he can pierce stone walls Madam, I am sure.

Cat. Direct *Don Valasco* hither by the backe staires,
I expect him.

Ans. I shall Madam.

Cat. Ha, whats this? a Letter to *Berinthia*, from whom
Subscrib'd? *Antonio*, what devill brought this hither?
Furies torment me not, ha, while I am *Antonio*, expect
Not I can be other then thy servant, all my thoughts
Are made sacred with thy remembrance, whose hope
Sustaines my life, oh I drink poyson from these fatall accents,
Be thy soule blacker then the inke that staines
The cursed paper, would each droppe had falne
From both your hearts, and every Character
Beene tex'd with blood, I would have tir'd mine eyes
To have read you both dead here, upon my life
Diego hath beene the cunning Mercury
In this conveyance, I suspect his love
Is but a property to advance this suite.
But I will crosse um all;   *Enter Valasco.*
Don Valasco, you are seasonably arriv'd,
I have a Letter for you.

Val. For me?

Cata. It does concerne you.   *Val.* Ha

Cata. How doe you like it sir?

Val. As I should a Punyard sticking here, how came
You by it?

Cata. I found it here by accident oth' ground,
I am sure it did not grow there, I suppose
Diego, the servant of *Antonio*
Who colourably pretends affection

To

To *Anſilva*, brought it, hees the agent for him,
Now the deſigne appeares, day is not more conſpicuous
Then this cunning.

   Val. I am reſolv'd.   *Cat.* For what?

   Val. Antonio or I muſt change our ayre,
This is beyond my patience ſleepe in this
And never woke to honour, oh my fates,
He takes the freehold of my ſoule away,
Berinthia, and it, are but one creature,
I have beene a tame foole all this while,
Swallowed my poyſon in a fruiteleſſe hope,
But my revenge, as heavy as *Ioves* wrath,
Wrapt in a thunderbolt is falling on him.

   Cat. Now you appeare all nobleneſſe, but collect
Draw up your paſſions to a narrow point
Of vengeance, like a burning glaſſe that fires
Sureſt ith ſmalleſt beame, he that would kill,
Spends not his idle fury to make wounds,
Farre from the heart of him he fights withall,
Looke where you moſt can danger, let his head
Bleed out his braines, or eyes, aime at that part
Is deereſt to him, this once put to hazzard,
The reſt will bleed to death.

   Val. Apply this Madam.

   Cat. The time invites to action, ile be briefe,
Strike him through *Berinthia*.   *Val.* Ha.

   Cat. Miſtake me not, I am her ſiſter,
Shee is his heart, make her your owne, you have
A double victory, thus you may kill him
With moſt revenge, and give your owne deſires,
A moſt confirm'd poſſeſſion, fighting with him,
Can be no conqueſt to you, if you meane
To ſtrike him dead, purſue *Berinthia*,
And kill him with the wounds he made at you,
It will appeare but juſtice, all this is
Within your fathom ſir.

   Val. Tis ſome divinity hangs on your tongue.

   Cat. If you conſent *Berinthia* ſhall not ſee,

       More

More sunnes till you enjoy her.

    Val. How deere Madam,

   Cat. T. us, you shall steale her away.

    Val. Oh when ?   *Cat.* Provide

Such trusty friends, but let it not be knowne

Vpon your honour, I assist you in't.

And after midnight when soft sleepe hath charm'd

All sences, enter the Garden gate.

Which shall be open for you, to know her chamber

A candle shall direct you in the Window,

Ansilva shall attend too, and provide

To give you entrance, thence take *Berinthia,*

And soone convey her to what place you thinke

Secure and most convenient, in small time

You may procure your owne conditions;

But sir you must engage your selfe to use her

With honourable respects, she is my sister,

Did not *I* thinke you noble, for the world

I would not runne that hazzard.

   Val. Let heaven forsake me then, was ever mortall

So bound to womans care, my mothers was

Halfe paid her at my birth, but you have made me

 An everlasting debtor.

  Cat. Select your friends, bethinke you of a place

You may transpose her.

   Val. I am all wings.   *Exit*

   Cat. So, when gentle physicke will not serve, we must

Apply more active, but there is

Yet a receipt behind; V*alascoes* shallow,

And will be planet strucke, to see *Berinthia*

Dye in his armes: tis so, yet he himselfe

Shall carry the suspition, if art,

Or hell can furnish me with such a poyson,

Sleepe thy last sister, whilst thou livest I have,

No quiet in my selfe, my rest thy grave.   *Exit*

     Diego comes from behinde the hangings.

  Die. Goe thy wayes, and the devill wants a breeder thou

                              Art

Art for him, onē spirit and her selfe are able to furnish
Hell and it were unprovided; but I am glad I heard all,
I shall love hangings the better while I live:
I pereeive some good may be done behind em,
But ile acquaint my Lady *Berinthia,*
Heres her chamber I obferv'd: Madam, Madam
Berinthia.   *Berinthia above.*

  Ber. Whofe there?

  Die. Tis I *Diego,* I am *Diego.*

  Ber. Honeft *Diego,* what good newes,

  Die. Y are undone, undone loft, undone for ever; it is timē
now to be ferious.

  Ber. Ha,

  Die. Wheres my Mafter *Antonioes* Letter.

  Ber. Here, where, ha, alas, I feare I have loft it.

  Die. Alas you have undone your felfe, and your fifter, my
Lady *Catalina* hath found ir, and is mad with rage, and envy
againft you; I overheard your deftruction, fhe hath fhewed
it to *Don Valafco,* and hath plotted that he fhall fteale you a-
way this night, the doores fhall be left open the houre after
twelve.

  Ber. You amaze me, tis impoffible.

  Die. Doe not caft away your felfe, by incredulity, upon my
life your fate is caft, nay more, worfe then that.

  Ber. Worfe?

  Die. You muft be poyfoned too, oh fhees a cunning devill,
and fhe will carry it fo, that *Valafco* fhall bee fufpected for
your deat), what will you doe?

  Ber. I am overcome with amazement?

  Die. Madam remember with what noble love my Mafter
Antonio does honour you, and now both fave your felfe, and
make him happy, how.

  Ber. I am loft man.

  Die. Feare not, I will engage my life for your fafety,
Seeme not to have knowledge or fufpicion, be carefull
What you receive, leaft you be poyfon'd, leave the
Reft to me, I have a crotchet in my pate fhall fpoyle
Their muficke, and prevent all danger I warrant you,

By any meanes be smooth, and pleasant, the devils
A knave, your sisters a Traytor, my Master is your noble
Friend, I am your honest servant, and *Valasco* shall
Shake his eares like an annimall.

Ber. It is not to be hoped for.

Die. Then cut of my eares, slit my nose, and make a devill
of me, shall I about it say, tis done.

Ber. Any thing thou art honest, heaven be neare,
Still to my innocence, I am full of feare.

Die. Spurre cut and away then.   *Exeunt*

   Enter Signior Sharkino in his study furnished with glasses,
     viols, pictures of wax characters, wands, conju-
       ring habit, Powders paintings, and Scarabeo.

Sh. Scarabeo.   *Sca.* Sir.

Sh. Is the doore tongue tide, scrue your selfe halfe out at
one of the crevices, and give me notice what patient approa-
ches me.

Sca. I can runne through the key hole sir.

Sh. This *fucus* beares
A lively tincture, oh the cheeke must blush
That weares it, their deceiv'd that say
Art is the ape of nature.   *Sca.* Sir.

Sh. Who ist?

Sca. My Ladies apron strings, Mistris *Ansilva* her chamber-
maide.   *Sh.* Admit her.

       Enter Ansilva.

Ans. How now raw head and bloody bones, wheres the
Doctor *Sharkino?* oh here he is.

Sh. How does your vertuous Ladie.

Ans. In good health sir.
Wheres the *Fucus,* and the Powder.

Sh. All is prepared here.

Ans. To see what you can doe, many make legges, and you
make faces sir.

Sh. Variety of faces is now in fashion, and all little enough
for some to set a good face on't, oh Ladies may now and then
commit a slip, and have some colour for't, but these are but
the out sides of our art, the things we can prescribe to be ta-
                        k en

ken inwardly, are pretty curiofities, we can prolong life.

Anf. And kill too can you not ?

Sh. Oh any that will goe to the price.

Anf. You have poyfons I warrant you, how doe they looke, pray lets fee one.

Sh. Oh naturall, and artificiall. *Neffas* blood was milke
To em, an extraction of Todes and Vipers, looke
Heres a parcell of *Claudius Cæfars* poffet,
Given him by his wife *Agrippina*, here is fome of
Hannibals medicine he carried alwaies in the
Pummell of his fword, for a dead lift, a very active
Poyfon, which paffing the *Orifice*, kindles
Straite a fire, inflames the blood, and makes the marrow
Fry, have you occafion to apply one.

Anf. Introth we are troubled with a rat in my Ladies
Chamber.

Sh. A Rat, give him his bane, would you deftroy a City, I
have *probatinm* of *Italian* Sallets, and our owne Country figs
fhall doe it rarely, a Rat, I have fcarfe a poyfon fo bafe, the
worft is able to kill a man, I have all forts, from a minute to
feven yeares in operation, and leave no markes behinde em, a
Rats a Rat.

Anf. Pray let me fee a remover at twelve houres, and I would
be loath to kill the poore thing prefently.

Sh. Here, you may caft it away upon't, but tis a difparage-
ment to the poyfon.

Anf. This will content you.

Sh. Becaufe it is for a Rat you fhall pay no more, my fer-
vice to my Ladie, my poyfons howfoever I give them, variety
of operations are all but one.   *Knockes within.*
Honeft Rats bane in feverall fhapes, their vertue is common,
and will not be long in killing; you were beft looke it be a
Rat, *Scarabeo.*

Sca. Sir heres a Gallant enquires for Doctor *Sharkino.*

Sh. Vfher him in, it is fome *Don.*

Enter Count de Monte Nigro.

Count. Is your name *Signior Sharkino* the famous Doctor.
                                        Sh. They

Sh. They call me *Sharkino.*

Count. Doe you not know me?

Sh. Your gracious pardon.

Count. I am *Count de Monte Nigro.*

Sh. Your honours sublimity doth illustrate this habitation;
Is there any thing wherein *Sharkino* may expresse
His humble service? if ought within the circumference
Of a Medicinall or Mathematicall science,
May have acceptance with your celsitude,
It shall devolve it selfe.

Coun Devolve it selfe, that word is not in my Table bookes,
what are all these trinkets?

Sh. Take heede I beseech your honour, they are dangerous,
this is the devils girdle.

Coun. A pox oth devill, what have I doe with him,

Sh. It is a dreadfull circle of conjuration, fortified
With sacred characters against the power
Of infernall spirits, within whose round I can tread
Safely, when hell burnes round about me.

Coun. Not unlikely.

Sh. Will you see the devill sir?

Coun. Ha, the devill? not at this time, I am in some hast,
Any thing but the devill I durst fight with all, harke
You Doctor, letting these things passe, hearing
Of your skill, I am come in my owne person, for
A fragment of your art, harke you, have you any
Receipts to procure love sir?

Sh. All the degrees of it this is ordinary.

Coun. Nay I would not have it too strong, the Lady I in-
tend it for, is pretty well taken already, an easing working
thing does it.

Sh. Heres a powder whose ingrediences were fetch'd
From *Arabia* the happy, a sublimation of the Phœnix
Ashes, when she last burned her selfe, it beates the
Colour of sinamon, two or three scruples put into
A cup of wine, fetches up her heart she can scarse
Keepe it in, for running out of her mouth to you
My noble Lord.

Count.

Count. That, let me have that, Doctor I know tis deare,
Will that gold buy it?

Sh. Your honour is bountifull, there needs no circumstance,
Minister it by whom you please, your intention binds it to
operation.

Cou. So, so *Catalina*, I will put your mornings draught
In my pocket———*Knocke at the doore*
Doctor, I would not be seene.

Sh. Please you my Lord obscure your selfe behinde these
hangings then, till they be gone, Ile dispatch 'em the sooner;
or if your honour thinke fit, tis but clouding your person with
a simple cloake of mine, and you may at pleasure passe without discovery, my Anotomy shall waite on you.

Enter three Servingmen.

1 Prethee come backe yet.

2 Oh by any meanes goe *Iaynes*.

1 Dost thou thinke it possible that any man can tell where
thy things are, but he that stole 'em, hee's but a jugling impo-
ster, a my conscience, come backe againe.

2 Nay now wee are at furthest, be not rul'd by him, I
know he is a cunning man, he told me my fortune once when
I was to goe a journey by water, that if I scapt drowning, I
should doe well enough, and I have liv'd ever since.

3. Well I will try, I am resolv'd; stay, here hee is *Pedro*,
you are acquainted with him, breake the ice, he is alone.

2. Blesse you Mr. Doctor; sir presuming on your Art, here
is a fellow of mine, indeede the Butler, for want of a better;
has lost a dozen of Dyaper spoones, and halfe a dozen of silver Napkins yesterday, they were seene by all three of us in
the morning betweene sixe and seven set up, and what spirit
of the Buttery hath stollen 'em before eight, is invisible to our
understanding.

3 He hath delivered you the case right, I beseech you sir
doe what you can for a servant, that is like to be in a lamenta-
ble case else, here's a gratuity.

1. Now we shall see what the devill can do, hey, heres one
of his spirits I thinke.

Sh. Betweene 7 and 8. the houre; the 1 *Luna*, the 2 *Sa-*

F   *turne*

turne, the 3 *Iupiter,* the 4 *Mars,* the 5 *Sol,* the 6 *Venus,* the 7 *Mercury,* ha then it was stolne, *Mercury* is a thiese, your goods are stolne.

3 Was *Mercury* the thiefe, pray where dwells he?

Sh. *Mercury* is above the Moone man.

3. Alas sir tis a great way thither.

1. Did not I tell you you would be gull'd.

Sh. Well y'are a servant, Ile doe something for you; What will you say, if I shew you the man that stole your Spoones and Napkins presently, will that satisfie you.

3 Ile desire no more, oh good Mr. Doctor.

1 If he does that, ile beleve he has cunning.

Sh. Goe to, heares a glasse.

2 Loe you there now.

Sh. Stand your backes North, and stirre not till I bid you; What see you there?

3 Heres nothing.

Sh. Looke agen, and marke, stand yet more North.

3 Now I see somebody.   1 And I.

The Count comes from behind the Hangings and muffled in a cloake steales of the Stage.

Sh. Marke this fellow muffled in the cloake, he hath stolne your spoones and Napkins, does he not skulke.

1 'Foote tis strange, he lookes like a theefe, this Doctor J see is cunning.

3. Oh rogue how shall's come by him, oh for an Officer.

Sh. Yet stirre not,

3. Oh hees gone, where is he?

Sh. Be not too rash, my Art tells me there is danger in't, you must be blinfold all, if you observe me not, all is to no purpose, you must not see till you be forth a doores, shut your eyes, and leade one another, when you are abroad open them, and you shall see agen.

3. The thiefe?

Sh. The same, then use your pleasures, so, be sure you see not, conduct them *Scarabeo.*   *Exeunt.*

Enter a Maid with an Urinall.

Ma. Oh Mr. Doctor I have got this opportunity to come

to.

to you, but I cannot stay, heres my water, pray sweet Mr. Doctor, tell me, I am in great feare that I have lost ----

Sh. What?

Ma. My maidenhead sir, you can tell by my water.

Sh. Dost not thou know?

Ma. Oh I doe somewhat doubt my selfe, for this morning when I rose, I found a paire of breeches on my bed, and I have had a great suspition ever since, it is an evill signe they say, and one does not know what may be in those breeches sometimes; sweete Mr. Doctor, am I a maid still or no, I would be sorry to loose my maidenhead ere I were aware, I feare I shall never be honest after it.

Sh. Let me see *Vrina meretrix* ; the colour is a strumpet, but the contents deceive not, your maidenhead is gone.

Ma. And is there no hope to finde it againe?

Sh. You are not every body, by my Art, as in other things that have beene stolne, he that hath stolne your maidenhead shall bring it againe.

Ma. Thanke you sweet Mr. Doctor, I am in your debt for this good newes; oh sweet newes sweet Mr. Doctor. *Exit.*

Enter Count beating before him the three Servingmen,
they runne in.

1 Cry your honour mercy, good my Lord.

Count. Out you slaves, oh my toes.

Sh. What ayles your Lordship?

Count. Doctor, I am out of breath, where be these wormes crept, I was never so abused since I was swadled : harke you, those 3. Rogues that were here even now, began to lay hold of me, and told me I must give them their Spoones and Napkins; they made a theefe of mee, but I thinke I have made their flesh jelly with kickes and bastinadoes; oh I have no mercy when I set on't, I have made e'm all poore *Iohns,* impudent varlets; talke to me of Spoones and Napkins.

Sh. Alas one of them was mad, and brought to me to cure him.

Count. Nay they were all mad, but I thinke I have madded e'm; I feare I have kickt two or three out of their lives; alas

poore

poore wretches I am sorry for it now, but I have such an humor of beating & kicking when my foote's in once: harke you Doctor, is it not within the compasse of your physicke to take downe a mans courage a thought lower; the truth is, I am apt of my selfe to quarrell upon the least affront ith' world, I cannot be kept in, chaines will not hold mee: t'other day for a lesse matter than this, I kickt halfe a dozen of high Germans, from one end of the streete to the other, for but offering to shrinke betweene mee and the wall; not aday goes o're my head but I hurt some body mortally; poxe a these rogues, I am sorry at my heart I have hurt e'm so, but I cannot forbeare.

Sb. This is strange.

Count. How? I can scarce forbeare striking you now, for saying it is strange; you would not thinke it: oh the wounds I have given for a very looke; well, harke you, if it be not too late, I would be taken downe, but I feare 'tis impossible, and then every one goes in danger of his life by me.

Sb. Take downe your spirit, looke you, dee see this inch and a halfe, how tall a man doe you thinke he was? He was twelve cubits high, and three yards compasse at the waste when I tooke him in hand first, ile draw him through a ring ere I have done with him: I keepe him now to breake my poysons, to eate Spiders and Toades, which is the onely dish his heart wishes for; a Capon destroyes him, and the very sight of beefe or mutton makes him sicke; looke, you shall see him eate his supper, come on your wayes, what say you to this Spider? looke how he leapes.

Sca. Oh dainty.

Sb. Here, saw you that? how many legges now for the hanch of a Toade.

Sca. Twenty, and thanke you sir, oh sweete Toade, oh admirable Toade.

Count. This is very strange, I nere saw the like. I never keew Spiders and Toades were such good meates before; will he not burst now?

Sb. It shall nere swell him, by to morrow hee shall be an

inch

inch ab:ted, and I can with an other experiment plumpe
him and highten him at my pleasure; ile warrant ile take you
downe my Lord.

Count. Nay but dee here, doe I looke like a Spider-catcher,
or Toade-eater.

Sb. Farre be it from *Sharkino*, I have gentle pellets for your
Lordship, shall melt in your mouth, and take of your valour
insensibly; Lozenges that shall comfort your stomacke, and
but at a weeke restraine your fury two or three thoughts;
does your honour thinke I would forget my selfe. I shew you
by this Rat what I can doe by Art: yout Lordship shall have
an easie composition, ho hurt ith' world in't; here take
but halfe a dozen of these going to bed, e're morning it shall
worke gently, and in the vertue appeare every day after-
ward.

Count. But if I find my selfe breaking out into fury, I may
take e'm often; heres for your pellets of Lozenges, what
rare physicke is this? Ile put it in practise presently, farewell Doctor.   *Exit.*

Sb. Happinesse wait on your egregious Lordship, my physicke shall make your body soluble, but for working on your
spirit, beleeve it when you finde it; with any lies we must set
forth our simples and compositions to utter them: so this is a
good dayes worke; leane chaps lay up, and because you have
perform'd hamsomly, there is some silver for you, lay up my
properties: Tis night already, thus we knaves will thrive,
when honest plainnesse know not how to live.

                                                         Exeunt.

Enter Catalina and Ansilva.

Cat. Art sure she has tane it?

Ans. As sure as I am alive? she never eate with
Such an appetite, for I found none left, I would
Be loath to have it so sure in my belly, it will worke
Rarely twelve houres hence.

Cata. Thus we worke sure then, time runnes upon
Th'appointed houre, *Valasco* should rid me of all my

Feares.

Feares at once, upon thy life be carefull to direct
Him at his first approach, I am sicke till she
Be delivered; be secret as the night, ile to my
Chamber, be very carefull.

   Enter Antonio, Villandras, Diego, vizzarded and arm'd.

Ant. Art sure thou hast the time right.

Die. Doubt not, yonder's her chamber, the light
speakes it; softly.

   Ans. Whose there ? *Vallasco* ?   *Ant.* I.

   Ans. That way, make no noise, things are prepared, softly
So, so, this is good I hope and weight too, my Lady
Berinthia will be sure enough anon, I shall nere
Get more higher, I had much adoe to perswade her
To the spice, but I swore it was a cordiall my Lady
Vs'd her selfe, and poore foole she has swallowed it
Sure.   *Enter Ant. with Berinthia, Villan. Diego.*

   Ant. Madam feare not I am your friend.

   Die. Who are you ?

   Vill. Stop her mouth, away.   *Exeunt.*

     Enter Ansilua.

   Ans. So, so they are gone, alas poore *Valasco* I pitty thee,
But we creatures of polliticke Ladies must hold the
Same byas with our Mistresses, and tis some pollicy
To make them respect us the better, for feare our
Teeth be not strong enough to keepe in our tongues:
Now must I study out some tale by morning to salute
My old Lord withall.

     Enter Velisco, a friend or two armed.

   Val. Ansilua ?   *Ans.* Some body calls me, who is it ?

   Val. It is I *Valasco*

   Ans. What comes he backe for ? I hope the poyson does
Not worke already, where have you dispos'd her.

   Val. Dispos'd whom ?

   Ans. My Lady *Berinthia.*

   Val. Let me alone to dispose her, prethee where's the light?
Shew us the way.

   Ans. What way ?

   Val. The way to her chamber ? come, I know what
                           Ycu

You are ficke of, here each minute is an age till
I poffeffe *Berinthia.*

   Anf. This is pretty, I hope my Lady is well.

   Val. Well?

   Anf. My Lady *Berinthia* fir.

   Val. Doe you mocke me?

   Anf. I mocke you?

   Val. I fhall grow angry, lead me to
Berinthias chamber, or ——

   Anf. Why fir, were not you here even now, and hurried
Her away, I have your gold well fare all good tokens;
I have perform'd my duty already fir, and you had my
Lady.

   Val. I am abus'd you are a cunning Devill, I heare and had
Berinthia, tell me, or with this piftoll, I will foone
Reward thy treachery, wheres *Berinthia?*

   Anf. Oh I befeech you doe not fright me fo, if you were
Not here even now, here was another that call'd
Himfelfe *Valafco*, to whom I gave acceffe, and
He has carried her away.   *Exit.*

   Val. Am I awake? or doe I dreame this horrour:
Where am I? who does know me, are you friends
Of *Don Valafco?*

   1. Doe you doubt us fir?

   Val. I doubt my felfe, who am I

   2. Our noble friend *Valafco.*

   Val. Tis fo, I am *Valafco*, all the Furies
Circle me round, oh teach me to be mad,
I am abus'd, infufferably tormented,
My very foule is whipt, it had beene fafer
For *Catalina* to have plaid with Serpents.

        Enter Catalina and Anfilva.

   Cat. Thou talkeft of wonders, where is *Valafco?*

   Anf. He was here even now.

   Val. Who nam'd *Valafco?*

   Cata. Twas I, *Catalina*, here.

   Val. Could you picke none out of the ftocke of man
To mocke but me, fo bafely?

                         Cata.

Cata. *Valasco* be your selfe, resume your vertue,
My thoughts are cleare from your abuse, it is
No time to vent our passions, fruitlesse rages,
Some hath abus'd us both, but a revenge
As swift as lightning shall pursue their flight:
Oh I could seare my braines, as you respect
Your honoures safety, or *Berinthias* love;
Haste to your lodging, which being nere our house,
You shall be sent for; seeme to be rais'd up,
Let us alone to make a noise at home,
Fearefull as thunder; try the event, this cannot
Doe any hurt, you *Ansilva* shall
With clamors wake the houshold cunningly,
While I prepare my selfe.

  Val. I will suspend awhile.   *Exeunt.*

  Ans. Helpe, helpe, theeves, villaines, murder, my Lady:
Helpe oh my Lord, my Lady, murder, theeves, helpe.

        Enter Sebastiano in his shirt with a Taper.

  Seb. What fearefull cry is this, where are you?
  Ans. Here oh I am almost kil'd.
  Seb. *Ansilva* where art hurt?
  Ans. All over sir, my Lady *Berinthia* is carried away
By Ruffians, that broke into her chamber, alas
Sees gone.   *Seb.* Whether? which way?

        Enter Vilarezo Catalina.

My sister *Berinthia* is violently tane out of her
Chamber, and heres *Ansilva* hurt, see looke about,
Berinthia sister. *Cat.* How *Berin.* gone? call up the servants,
Ansilva, how wast?

  Ans. Alas Madam, I have not my senses about me, I am so
Frighted, vizards, and swords, and pistols, but my
Lady *Berinthia* was quickly seiz'd upon, shees gone.
  Vil. What villaines durst attempt it?

        Enter Count Monte de nigro with a torch.

I feare *Valasco* guilty of this rape.
  Cat. Runne one to his lodging presently, it will appeare
I know he lov'd her, oh my Lord, my sister *Berinthias* lost;
  Mont. How? foote my physicke begins to worke, ile come
to you presently.   *Exit.*   *Cat.*

Vil. Nor thinke my noble cozen meaneth you any dishonour here.

Ant. Dishonour, it is a language I never understood, yet
Throw off your feares *Berinthia*, yare ith' power
Of him that dares not thinke
The least dishonour to you.

Sfor. True by this buffe jerkin, that hath look'd ith face of
an Army, and he lies like a termagant, denies it, *Antonio* is
Lord of the Castle, but ile command fire to the gunnes, upon
any Renegado that confronts us, set thy heart at rest my gillo-
flower, we are all friends I warrant thee, and hees a Turke
that does not honour thee from the haire of thy head, to thy
pettitoes.

Ant. Come be not sad.

Cast. Put on fresh blood, yare not cheerefull, how doe you?

Ber. I know not how, nor what to answer you,
Your loves I cannot be ungratefull to,
Yare my best friends I thinke, but yet I know not
With what consent you brought my body hither.

Ant. Can you be ignorant what plot was laid
To take your faire life from you.

Ber. If all be not a dreame, I doe remember
Your servant *Diego* told me wonders, and
I owe you for my preservation, but——

Sfor. Shoote not at Buts, *Cupids* an archer, heres a faire
marke, a fooles bolts soone shot, my names *Sforza* still, my
double Daisie.

Cast. It is your happinesse you have escaped the malice of
your sister.

Vil. And it is worth
A noble gratitude to have beene quit,
By such an honourer as *Antonio* is
Of faire *Berinthia*.

Ber. Oh but my Father, under whose displeasure I ever
Ant. You are secure   (sinke.

Ber. As the poore Deere that being pursuid, for safety
Gets up a rocke that over hangs the Sea,
Where all that she can see, is her destruction,

Before

Before the waves, behinde her enemies
Promife her certaine ruine.

   Ant. Faine not your felfe fo haplefſe my *Berinthia,*
Raife your dejected thoughts, be merry, come,
Thinke I am your *Antonio.*

   Caſt. It is not wifdome
To let our paſſed fortunes trouble us,
Since were they bad, the memorie is fweete,
That we have paſt them, looke before you Lady,
The future moſt concerneth.

   Ber. You have awak'd me, *Antonio* pardon,
Vpon whofe honour I dare truſt my felfe,
I am refolv'd, if you dare keepe me here,
T'expect fome happier iſſue.

   Ant. Dare keepe thee here ? with thy confent, I dare
Deny thy Father, by this fword I dare,
And all the world.

   Sfor. Dare, what giant of vallour dares hinder us, from da-
ring to flit the weafands of them that dare fay, wee dare not
doe any thing, that is to be dared under the poles, I am old
Sforza, that in my dayes have fcoured rogues faces with hot
bals, made em cut croſſe capers, and fent them away with a
powder, I have a company of roring buls upon the wals, ſhall
ſpit fire in the faces of any ragamuffian that dares fay, we dare
not fight pell mell, and ſtill my name is *Sforza.*

         Enter Diego haſtily.

   Die. Sir your noble friend *don Sebaſtiano* is at the caſtle gate.

   Ant. Your brother Lady, and my honoured friend,
Why doe the gates not fpread themfelves, to open
At his arrivall *Sforza,* tis *Berinthiaes* brother,
Sebaſtiano the example of all worth
And friendfhip, is come after his fweete fifter,

   Ber. Alas I feare.

   Ant. Be not fuch a coward Lady, he cannot come
Without all goodneſſe waiting on him, *Sforza,*
Sforza I fay, what pretious time we lofe,
Sebaſtiano, I almoſt lofe my felfe
In joy to meete him, breake the iron barres.

                           And

And giue him entrance.

   Sfor. Ile breake the wals downe, if the gates be too little.

   Caſt. I much deſire to ſee him.

   Ant. Siſter, now hees come, he did promiſe me
But a ſhort abſence, he of all the world
I would call brother, *Caſtabella* more
Then for his ſiſters loue, oh hees a man
Made up of merit, my *Berinthia*
Throw off all cloudes, *Sebaſtianoes* come.

   Ber. Sent by my Father to——

   Ant. What, to ſee thee? he ſhall ſee thee here.
Reſpected like thy ſelfe, *Berinthia,*
Attended with *Antonio,* begirt with armies of thy ſeruants.

     Enter Sebaſtiano Mounte Nigro, Sforza.

Oh my friend.

   Seb. Tis yet in queſtion ſir, and will not be
So eaſily proued.

   Moun. No ſir, weele make you proue your ſelfe our friend.

   Ant. What face haue you put on? am I awake?
Or doe I dreame *Sebaſtiano* frownes.

   Seb. *Antonio* I come not now to Complement,
While you were noble, I was not leaſt of them
You cald your friends, but you are guilty of
An action that deſtroyes that name.

   Sfor. Bones a your Father, does he come to ſwagger,
My name is *Sforza* then.

   Ant. No more,
I guiltie of an action ſo diſhonourable
Has made me vnworthy of your friendſhip;
Come y'are not in earneſt, tis enough I know
My ſelfe *Antonio.*

   Seb. Adde to him vngratefull.

   Ant. Twas a foule breath deliuered it, and wert any
But *Sebaſtiano,* he ſhould feele the weight
Of ſuch a falſhood.

   Seb. Siſter you muſt along with me.

   Ant. Now by my Fathers ſoule, he that takes her hence
Vnleſſe ſhe giue conſent, treads on his graue,

Sebastiano, y'are unnoble then,
Tis I that said it.

 Mount. So it seemes.

 Seb. Antonio, for here I throw of all
The ties of love, I come to fetch a sister,
Dishonourably taken from her father,
Or with my sword to force thee render her:
Now if thou beest a Souldier redeliver,
Or keepe her with the danger of thy person,
Thou canst not be my brother, till we first
Be allied in blood.

 Ant. Promise me the hearing,
And that have any satisfaction,
Becomes my fame.

 Mount. So, so, he will submit himselfe, it will be our honor.

 Ant. Wert in your power, would you not account it
A pretious victory, in your sisters cause,
To dye your sword with any blood of him,
Sav'd both her life and honour?

 Seb. I were ungratefull.

 Ant. You have told your selfe, and I have argument to
prove this.

 Seb. Why would you have me thinke, my sister owes to
you such preservation?

 Ant. Oh *Sebastiana,*
Thou dost not thinke what devill lies at home
Within a sisters bosome, *Catalina,*
(I know not with what worst of envy) laid
Force to this goodly building, and through poyson
Had rob'd the earth of more then all the world,
Her vertue.

 Seb. You must not beate my resolution off
With these inventions sir.

 Ant. Be not cozend,
With your credulity, for my blood, I value it
Beneath my honour, and I dare by goodnesse,
In such a quarrell kill thee: but heare all,
And then you shall have fighting your heart full.

Valasco

Sebaſtiano will not be remiſſe,
A gentle nature is abus'd with tales,
Which they know how to colour ; heres the Count.

Enter Monte nigro ſweating.

Cat. How, the Count ? I ſent him thither to be rid on him;
The foole has better fortune than I wiſht him,
But now I ſhall heare that, which will more comfort me,
My ſiſters death moſt certainely.

Mont. My Lord, I have rid hard, read there, your ſonne
And daughter is well. *Cat.* Ha, well ?

Mount. Madam. *Cat.* How does my ſiſter ?

Mount. In good health, ſhe has commendations to you
In that letter. *Val.* And is *Antonio* living ?

Mount. Yes, and remembers his ſervice to you,

Val. Has he then yeelded up *Berinthia* ?

Mon. He will yeeld up his ghoſt firſt, I know not wē wērē
Going to fleſh baſte one another, I am ſure but the
Matter of fellony hangs ſtill, who will cut it downe ;
I know not, Madam theres notable matter againſt you.

Cat. Me ?

Mount. Vpon my honor there is, be not angry with mē,
No leſſe than theft and murder, that letter is charg'd
Withall, but you'le cleare all I make no queſtion, they
Talke of poyſoning. *Cat.* Am I betray'd ?

Mount. Well, I ſmell, I ſmell. *Cat.* What do you ſmell?

Mount It was but a tricke of theirs to ſave their lives,
For we were bent to kill all that came againſt us.

Vil. *Catalina* reade here, *Valaſco*, both of you,
And let me reade your faces, ha ? they wonder.

Val. Howes this, I ſteale *Berinthia* ?

Cat. I poyſon my ſiſter. *Val.* This doth amaze me.

Cat. Father, this letter ſayes I would have poyſoned my
poore ſiſter, innocence defend me.

Vil. It will, it ſhall, come J acquit you both,
They muſt not thus foole me.

Moun. Madam I thought as much, my minde gave mē, it
Was a lye, yes, you lookē like a poyſoner, as much
As I looke like a Hobby-horſe.

Cat.

Cat. Was ever honest love so abused, have I
So poore reward for my affection,

Vil. It shall be so.

Val. Madam I know not how the poyson came in, but I
Feare some have betraied our plot.

Cat. And how came you off my noble Count.

Mount. As you see without any wounds, but much against
My will I was but one, *Sebastiano,* that was the
Principall, tooke a demurre upon their allegation :
It seemes, and so the matter is rak'd up in the Embers.

Val. To make a greater fire, were you so cold
To credit his excuse, *Antonio,*
I should not have beene so frozen,
As you love honor and revenge, give me
Some interest now, and if I doe not
Shew my selfe faithfull, let *Valasco* have
No name within your memory, let me begge,
To be your Proxie sir, pitty such blood,
As yours should be ignobly cast away ;
Maddam speake for me.

Cat. No, J had rather lose this foole.

Mont. And you can get their consents.

Cat. You cannot sir in honour now goe backe,
J shall not thinke you love me, if my father
Point you such noble service to refuse it.

Mount. You heare what she sayes.

Vil. Count *Monte nigro.*

Val. I am all fire with rage.

Vil. *Valasco,* you may accompany the Count,
There may be imployment of your valour too ;
Tell me at your returne, whether my sonne
May prove a souldier, heres new warrant for
Antonioes death, if there be coldnesse urge it,
Tis my desire, ile study a better service.

Val. I shall.

Vil. Away then both, no complement, I wish you either
Had a Pegasus, be happy, my old bloud boyles, this
Must my peace secure, such sores as these must

Have a defperate cure.   *Exeunt.*

    Enter Sebaft. Caftab. Anton. Berinthia.

 Seb. This honor Madam of your felfe and brother,
Make me unhappy, when I remember, what
I came for, not to feaft thus but to fight.

  Caft. Pitty true friendfhip fhould thus fuffer.

  Ant. Ha? *Seb.* Muficke.

 Ant. Somë conceit of *Sforza* thë old Captaine,
Lets entertaine it, fome fouldiers device,

    A maske of Souldiers.

Godamercy *Sforza.*

 Sfor. To your ftations now my brave brats of Millitary
Difcipline, enough, *Sforza* honours you, looke to your
Charge Bullies, and be ready upon all occafions,
My invincible dub a dub knights of the Caftlë,
Qui vala. *Enter Mounte nigro, Valafco.*

 Val. We muft fpeake with *Don Sebaftiano.*

 Sfor. Muft? Th'art a Mufhrumpe, muftin the Caftle of *Eluas.*

   Monte nigro gives a letter.

 Ant. Friends; *Sforza.*

 Val. What, courting Ladies, by this timë 'twas ëxpëfted
You would have courted fame fir, and woed her to you;
You fhall know me better.

 Ant. I doubt you'le never be better; you fhall now owë më.
More than you fhall account for.

  Seb. Or elfe my curfe, that word cries out for death.

  Caft. My feates perplexe më. *Anto. & Seb. whifpers.*

 Val. Madam I doe wonder
You can forgët your honour, and reflect
On fuch unworthineffe, wherein hath *Valafco*
Shewed you leffe merit.

 Ber. Sir it becomes not me
To weigh your worths, nor would I learnë of you
How to preferve my honour.

  Seb. Sifter.

 Ant. Villandras.

 Seb. Then J muft take my leave, for I am fent for,
I am forry for your fate, Madam I am expefted.

      H 3

By a father, your vertue hath made me yours.

  Mount. Oh admirable phisitian!

  Ant. Sforza, there is no remedie, but by all honour doe it,
Sister, I am to waite on him, oh my poore girle
Berinthia, my soule be with thee, for a
Little time excuse my absence.

  Sfor. You may walke sir.

  Val. Antonio I must but now looke on, you were
Best take a course not to out live him.

        Exeunt Sforza, Villandras : and Ladies.

  Ant. Sebastiano, I know not with what soule
I draw my sword against thee

  Seb. Antonio I am driven in a storme
To split my selfe on thee, if not, my curse ----
We must on sir.

  Mount. Rare man of art *Sharkino.*

  Vil. Guard thee Count.

        Enter Sfor. Val. and Ladies above.

  Cast. Treacherous *Sforza*, hast thou brought us hither, to
be stroke dead?

  Mount. Hold Gentlemen, give me audience.

  Seb. Whats the matter my Lord.

  Mount. My fit is on me, tis so, I had forgot my selfe,
This is my ague day.   *Seb.* How?

  Mount. Yes a sextile ague, looke you, doe you not see me
shake, admirable Doctor, it wil be as much as my life is worth
if I should fight a stroke.

  Seb. Hell on such basenesse, weele engage no more,
Let our swords try it out.

  Val. Sebastiano hold, thart not so ill befriended,
Exchange a person, ile leape the battlement.

  Mount. Withall my heart, I am sorry it happens so un-
fortunately, oh rare phisitian!

  Vil. Good cozen grant it.

  Ant. What saies *Sebastiano.*

  Vil. I conjure you by all honour.

  Seb. It is granted: *Ber.* He shall not goe.

  Ant. Meete him my Lord, you will become his place of a
                  Specta.

Caſt. He that hath ſent you ſir this gift, did lovē you,
Youle ſay your ſelfe he did.

Seb. Ha, name him prethee.

Caſt. The friend I came from was *Antonio.*

Seb. Thou lyeſt, and thart a villane, who hath ſent thēē
To tempt *Sebaſtianoes* ſoule to act on thee
Another death, for thus afrighting me.

Caſt. Indeede I doe not mocke, nor come to afright you
Heaven knowes my heart, I know *Antonioes* dead,
But twas a gift he in his life deſign'd
To you, and I have brought it.

Seb. Thou doſt not promiſe cozēnage, what gift is it?

Caſt. It is my ſelfe ſir, while *Antonio* liv'd, I was his boy,
But never did boy looſe ſo kinde a Maſter, in his life he
Promiſed he would beſtow me, ſo much was his love
To my poore merit, on his deareſt friend,
And nam'd you ſir, if heaven ſhould point out
To overlive him, for he knew you would
Love mē the better for his ſake, indeed
I will be very honeſt to you, and
Refuſe no ſervice to procure your love
And good opinion to me.

Seb. Can it be
Thou wert his boy, oh thou ſhouldſt hate mē then,
Th'art falſe, I dare not truſt thee, unto him
Thou ſheweſt thee now unfaithfull to accept
Of me, I kild him thy Maſter, twas a friend
He could commit thee to, I onely was,
Of all the ſtocke of men his enemy,
His cruelleſt enemy.

Caſt. Indēede I am ſure it was, hē ſpokē all truth,
And had he liv.'d to have made his will, I know
He had bequeathed me as a legacy
To be your boy; alas I am willing ſir
To obey him in it, had he laid on mē
Command, to have mingled with his ſacrēd duſt,
My unprofitable blood, it ſhould have beene
A moſt glad ſacrifice, and 't had beene honour

To have done him such a duty sir, I know
You did not kill him with a heart of mallice,
But in contention with your very soule
To part with him.

   Seb. All is as true as Oracle by heaven,
Dost thou beleeve so?

   Cast. Indeede I doe.   *Seb.* Yet be not rash;
Tis no advantage to belong to me,
I have no power nor greatnesse in the Court,
To raise thee to a fortune, worthy of
So much observance as I shall expect
When thou art mine.

   Cast. All the ambition of my thoughts shall be
To doe my dutie sir.

   Seb. Besides, I shall afflict thy tendernesse
With sollitude and passion, for I am
Onely in love with sorrow, never merry,
Weare out the day in telling of sad tales,
Delight in sighes and teares; sometimes I walke
To a Wood or River purposely to challenge
The bouldest Eccho, to send backe my groanes
Ith' height I breake e'm, come I shall undoe thee.

   Cast. Sir, I shall be most happy to beare part
In any of your sorrowes, I nere had
So hard a heart but I could shed a teare
To beare my Master company.

   Seb. I will not leave thee if thou'lt dwell with me
For wealth of *Indies*, be my loved boy,
Come in with me, thus Ile begin to do
Some recompence for dead *Antonio.*   *Enter Berinthia.*

   Ber. So I will dare my fortune to be cruell,
And like a mountanous peece of earth that suckes
The balls of hot Artillery, I will stand
And weary all the gunshot; oh my soule
Thou hast beene too long icy Alpes of snow;
Have buried my whole nature, it shall now
Turne Element of fire, and fill the'ayre
With bearded Comets, threatning death and horrour

For my wrong'd innocence, contemn'd, difgrac'd,
Nay murther'd, for with *Antonio*
My breath expired, and I but borrow this
To coart revenge for juſtice, if there be
Thoſe furies which doe waite on deſperate mēn,
As ſome have thought, and guide their hands to miſchieſe ;
Come from the wombe of night, aſſiſt a maide
Ambitious to be made a monſter like you ;
I will not dread your ſhapes, I am diſpos'd
To be at friendſhip with you, and want nought
But your blacke aide to ſcale it.

Enter Mounte Nigro and Anſilva.

Mount. Firſt ile locke up thy   *Gives her gold.*
Tongue, and tell thee my honorable meaning, ſo,
To tell you the truth, it is a love-potwder, I had it of the
Brave Doctor, which I would have thee to ſuger
The Ladies cup withall, for my ſake wo't do't ;
And if I marry her, ſhat find me a noble
Maſter, and thou ſhalt be my chiefe Gentlewoman
In Ordinary ; keepe thy body looſe, and thou ſhalt
Want no gowne I warrant thee; wo't do't.

Anſ. My Lord, I thinke my Lady is much taken with your
worth already, ſo that this will be ſuperfluous,

Mount. INay think ſhe has cauſe enough, but I have a great
Mind to make an end on't, to tell you true, there are
Halfe a dozen about mee, but I had rather ſhe ſhould have
Me than an other; and my blood is growne ſo boyſterous
For my body, thats another thing ; ſo that if thou wilt
Doe it *Anſilva*, thou wilt doe thy Lady good ſervice,
And live in the favour of *Count de Monte Nigro* ;
I will make thy children kinne to me, if thou wo't
Do't.   *Anſ.* I am your honours handmaid, but —

Mount. Heres a Diamond, prethee weare it, be not modeſt.

Anſ. 'Tis done my Lord, urge it no further.

Mount. But be ſecret too for my honors ſake, wē great mēn
Doe not love to have our actions laid open to the
Broad face of the world, Ile get thee with child,
And marry thee to a Knight, my brave *Anſilva*, takē

Thē firſt opportunity.

Anſ. Jf there be any vertue in thē powder, preparē to
Meete your wiſhes my noble Lord.

Moun. Thy *Count de monte nigro* expeĉt to be a Lady. *Exit.*

Ber. Anſilva. Anſ. Madam.

Ber. Nay you neede not hide it, I heard the conference,
And know the vertue of the powder, let me ſee it
Or ile diſcover all. *Anſ.* I am undone.

Ber. No, here take it againē, ile not prevent
My ſiſters happineſſe and the Counts deſire,
I am no Tell-tale good *Anſilva* giv't her,
And heavens ſucceede the operation,
I begge on my knee ; feare not *Anſilva*,
I am all ſilence. *Exit.*

Anſ. Indeede Madam, then ſhee ſhall havē it preſently.
Exit.

Enter Sebaſtiano, Caſtabella.

Caſt. Sir, if the opportunity I uſe
To comfort you be held a fault, and that
I keepe not diſtance of a ſervant, lay it
Vpon my love ; indeede if it be an errour
It ſprings out of my duty.

Seb. Prethee boy be patient ;
The more I ſtrive to throw off thē remembrance
Of dead *Antonio*, love ſtill rubbes the wounds
To make them bleede afreſh.

Caſt. Alas they are paſt,
Binde up your owne for honours ſake,
And ſhew love to your ſelfe, pray do not loſe your reaſon,
To make your griefe ſo fruitleſſe ; I have procur'd
Some muſicke ſir to quiet thoſe ſad thoughts,
That makes ſuch warre within you.

Seb. Alas good boy, it will but adde more weights
Of dulneſſe on me, I am ſtung with worſe
Than the *Tarantula*, to be cur'd with muſicke
'T has the exacteſt unity, but it cannot,
Accord my thoughts.

Caſt. Sir this your couch

Scēmēs

Seemes to invite so small repose;
Oh I beseech you taste it, ile begge
A little leave to sing;   *She sings*

Enter Berinthia.

Sweete sleepe charme his sad sences, and gentle
Thoughts let fall your flowing numbers, here and round
About hover cælestiall Angels with your wings,
That none offend his quiet, sleepe begins
To cast his nets o're me too, ile obey,
And dreame on him, that dreames not what I am.

Ber. Nature doth wrestle with me, but revenge
Doth arme my love against it, justice is
Above all tie of blood *Sebastiano*
Thou art the first shalt tell *Antonioes* ghost
How much I lov'd him.

She stabbes him upon his couch, Castab. rises and runnes in.

Seb. Oh stay thy hand *Berinthia*? no
Th'ast don't, I wish thee heavens forgivenesse, I cannot
Tarry to heare thy reasons, at many doores,
My life runnes out, and yet *Berinthia*
Doth in her name give me more wounds then these,
Antonio, oh *Antonio*, we shall now
Be friendes againe.   *Dies.*

Ber. Hees dead, and yet I live, but not to fall
Lesse then a constellation, more flames must
Make up the fire that *Berinthia*
And her revenge, must bathe in.

Enter Catalina poysoned, pulling Ansilva by the haire.

Cast. *Sebastiano*, sister.   *Ans.* murder.

Cat. Theres wild-fire in my bowells, sure I am poysoned,
Oh *Berinthia*.   *Ber.* Ha, ha.

Cat. Helpe mē to teare *Ansilva*, I am poysoned by
The Count and this fury.

Ber. Ha, ha.   *Cat.* Doe you laugh hereat.

Ber. Yes queene of hell to see thee
Sinke in the glory of thy hope for blisse:
But art sure th'art poysoned, ha?

Ans. Nay I have my part on't, I did but sip, and my belly

I 3   swells

Swells too; call you this love-powder, *Count Monte*
Nigro hath poyſoned us both.

   Ber. Y'are a paire of witches, and becauſe
Ile keepe your potion working, know y'are both
Poyſon'd by me, by me *Berinthia,*
Being thus tormented with my wrongs,
I arm'd my ſelfe with all proviſion
For my revenge, and had in readineſſe
That faithfull poyſon which ith' opportunity
I put upon *Anſilva* for the exchange
Of the amorous powder; oh fooles, my ſoule
Raviſh thy ſelfe with laughter, politiſion
My eldeſt divell ſiſter, does the heate
Offend your ſtomacke, troth charity, a little charitie
Th'onely Antidote, thats cold enough :
Looke heres *Sebaſtiano* ;
Now horrour ſtrike thy ſoule, to whoſe feareleſſe heart
I ſent this punyard, for *Antonioes* death;
And if that peece of thy damnation
Anſilva had not don't, I meant to have writ
Revenge with the ſame point upon thy breaſt;
But I doe ſurfeit in this brave prevention:
Sleepe, ſleepe *Antonioes* aſhes, and now ope
Thou marbell cheſt to take *Berinthia*
To mingle with his duſt.   *Wounds her ſelfe.*
    Cat. I have not ſo much heart as to curſe, muſt I die?
       Enter *Vilarezo, Caſtabella, Monte Nigro.*
    Caſt. Here my Lord, alas hees dead, my *Sebaſtiano*
    Vil. Catalina.   *Cat.* I am poyſon'd.
    Vil. Ha, Defend good heaven, by whom.
    Anſ. I am poyſoned too.
    Vil. Racke not my ſoule amazement, tis a dreame ſure.
    Anſ. Your Love-powder hath poyſoned us both.
    Mon. What will become of me now, I would I were hang'd
To be out of my paine, by this fleſh, as I am a Count.
I bought it of the Doctor for good love-powder;
But Madam I hope you are not poyſoned in earneſt.
    Cat. The devill on your fooleſhip, oh I muſt walke

                                   The

The darke foggy way that spits fire and brimstone,
No physicke to restore me? send for *Sharkino*, a cooler
A cooler, theres a Smiths forge in my belly, and the
Devill blowes the Bellowes, Snow-water, *Berinthia*
Has poysned me, sinke by mine owne engine;
I must hence, hence, farewell, will you let me die so?
Confusion, torment, death, hell.

    Mount. I am glad with all my heart that *Berinthia* has
Poysoned her, yet ——

    Ber. Oh it becomes thee bravely, heare me sir.
Antonioes death and my dishonours now
Have just revenge; I stabb'd *Sebastiano*, poysoned my sisters,
Oh but they made too soone a fury of me,
And split the patience, from whose dreadfull breach
Came these consuming fires, your passions fruitlesse;
My soule is reeling forth I know not whether;
Oh father my heart weepes teares, for you I dye, oh see.
A maides revenge with her owne Tragedy.

    Cat. *Ansilva*, oh thou dull wretch, hell on thy cursed
Weakenesse, thou gavest me
The poyson, but I licke earth, hold, a gentleman
Vsher to support me, oh I am gone, the poyson
Now hath torne my heart in peeces, *Moritur.*

    Vil. I am Planet strucke, a direfull Tragedy, and have
I no part in't: how doe you like it, ha? wast not
Done toth' life? they are my owne children; this was
My eldest girle, this *Berinthia* the Tragedian,
Whose love by me resisted, was mother of all this
Horror; and theres my boy too, that slew *Antonio*
Valiantly, and fell under his sisters rage, what
Art thou boy?

    Cast. Ile tell you now I am no boy,
But haplesse *Castabella*, sister to
The slaine *Antonio*, I had hop'd to have
Some recompence by *Sebastianoes* love,
For whose sake in disguise I thus adventur'd.
To purchase it, but death hath ravisht us,
And here I bury all my joyes on earth.

    Mount.

Mount. Sweet Lady, here's *Count de Monte nigro* alive
To be your servant.

Cast. Hence dull greatnesse.

Vil. Were you a friend of *Sebastiano* then?

Cast. Ile give you testimony.

Vil. No, I beleeve you, but thou canst not be my daughter;
Tis false, he lies that sayes *Beriathia*
Was author of their deathes, 'twas *Villarezo*,
A fathers wretched curiosity, dead, dead, dead.

Cast. And I will leave the world too, for I meane
To spend the poore remainder of my dayes
In some Religious house, married to heaven,
And holy prayers for *Sebastianoes* soule,
And my lost brother.

Vil. Will you so?

Cast. I pray let *Castabella* have the honour
To enshrine his bones, and when my breath expires,
For sorrow promiseth I shall not live
To see more Sunnes, let me be buried by him
As neere as may be possible, that in death
Our dust may meete, oh my *Sebastiano*,
Thy wounds are mine.

Vil. Come I am arm'd, take up their bodies, *Castabella* you
Are not chiefe mourner here, he was my sonne,
Remember that, *Berinthia* fast, she was the
Youngest, put her inh' pithole first, then *Catalina*;
Strow, strow flowers enough upon em, for they
Were maides; now *Sebastiano*, take him
Vp gently, he was all the sonnes I had; now
March, come you and I are twinnes in this dayes
Vnhappinesse, wee'le march together, follow close
Wee'le overtake em, softly, and as we go,
Wee'le dare our fortune for another woe.

FINIS.

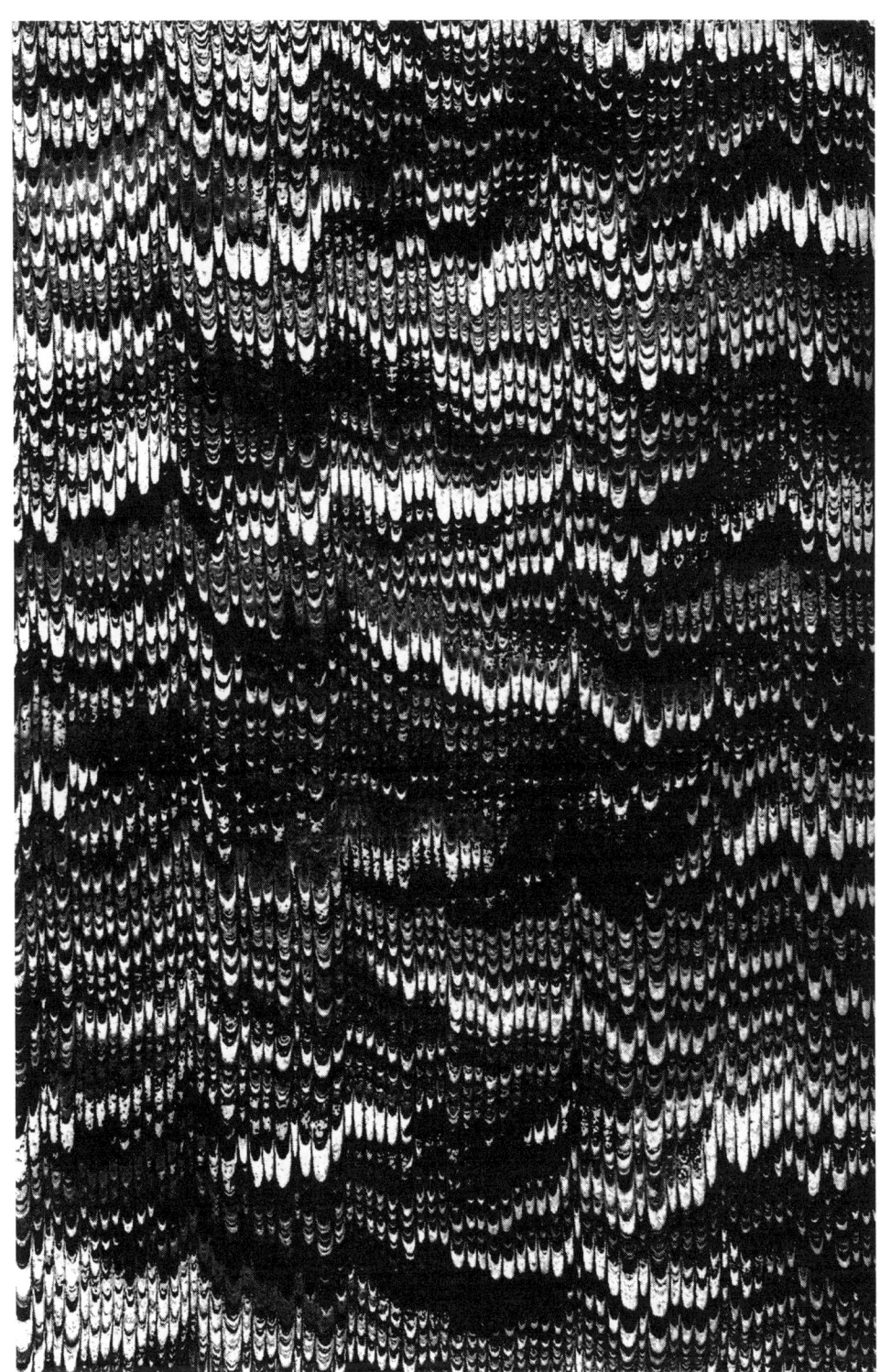

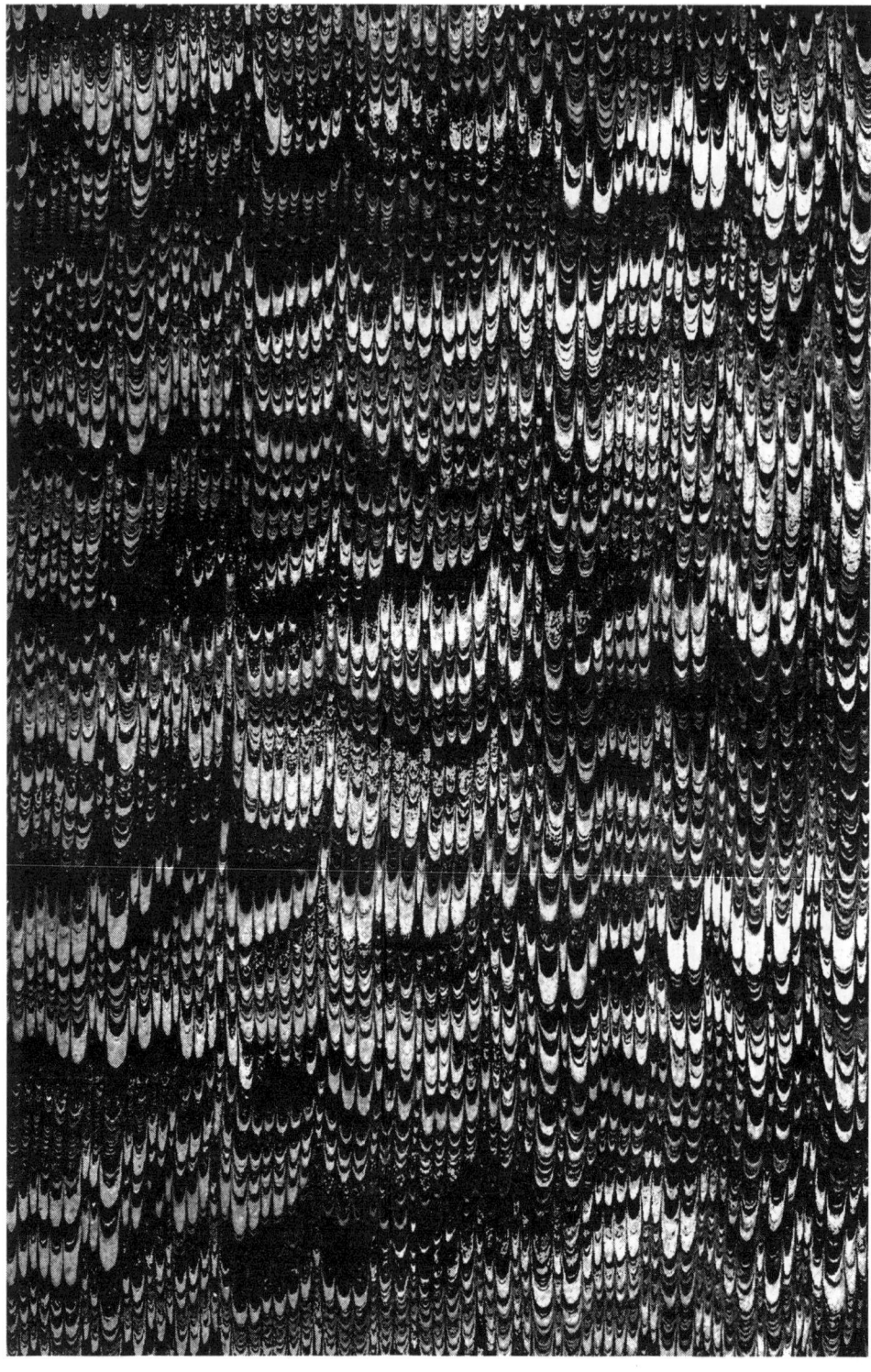

Lightning Source UK Ltd.
Milton Keynes UK
UKHW051253150123
415391UK00016B/166